CRAFTSMAN®

ROUTER
TECHNIQUES

An In-depth Guide to Using Your Router

by Philip Schmidt

CREATIVE PUBLISHING international

CHANHASSEN, MINNESOTA

www.creativepub.com

© Copyright 2004
Creative Publishing international, Inc.
18705 Lake Drive East
Chanhassen, Minnesota 55317
1-800-328-3895
www.creativepub.com

Printed by Quebecor World
10 9 8 7 6 5 4 3 2 1

President/CEO: Ken Fund
Vice President/Publisher: Linda Ball
Vice President/Retail Sales & Marketing: Kevin Haas

Executive Editor: Bryan Trandem
Creative Director: Tim Himsel
Managing Editor: Michelle Skudlarek
Editorial Director: Jerri Farris

Author: Philip Schmidt
Editor: Karen Ruth
Technical Photo Editor: Randy Austin
Art Director: Jon Simpson
Illustrator: Jon Simpson
Photo Researcher: Julie Caruso
Studio Services Manager: Jeanette Moss McCurdy
Photographers: Tate Carlson, Joel Schnell
Scene Shop Carpenters: Glen Austin, Randy Austin
Director of Production Services and Photography: Kim Gerber

ROUTER TECHNIQUES

CONTENTS

INTRODUCTION

The router's basic design has changed little over its 100 year history, yet it remains a very popular woodworking power tool. And the reason is simple: versatility. With its unparalleled accuracy and the thousands of bits it can use, the router has more capability than any other portable power tool. This book takes a straightforward approach to teaching you about routers, bits, and most importantly, using your router to its greatest potential.

For those new to the subject, Chapter 1 gives an overview of the main functions of a router, as well as a shopping guide covering what to look for when buying a new tool and accessories. You'll also find plenty of maintenance tips for ensuring top performance. Chapter 2 is devoted entirely to router bits and includes the information you need to find the best bits for the work you do and to get the most for your money.

From basic safety to tool setup and test cuts, you'll learn the essentials of routing technique in Chapter 3. Chapter 4 explores the router as a stationary tool. By mounting your router upside down beneath a flat table, you can make it perform like a shaper, jointer, or even a table saw.

The final chapters of the book focus on the main functions of hand-held and table routing. You'll learn edge-forming techniques for creating sculpted edges, guide routing setups for cutting flawless grooves and slots, jig options for making traditional joinery, and template routing for duplicating any shape.

Once you give it a spin, you're sure to agree with the millions of woodworkers who name the router as their favorite all-around tool. And *Router Techniques* has the information and answers you need to get the most out of your router.

NOTICE TO READERS

This book provides useful instructions, but we cannot anticipate all of your working conditions or the characteristics of your materials and tools. For safety, you should use caution, care, and good judgment when following the procedures described in this book. Always read and understand the owner's manual for your router and other power tools. Consider your own skill level and the instructions and safety precautions associated with the various tools and materials shown. The publisher cannot assume responsibility for any damage to property, injury to persons, or losses incurred as a result of misuse of the information provided.

CRAFTSMAN

Switch back and forth between
regular routing and plunge
routing simply by interchanging
bases quickly and easily!

9.5 Amp 2 Peak HP motor

Single speed 25,000 RPM
(no-load speed)

1/4-in. Collet

10 ft. Cord

Two Interch

Includes Hea

1/4-in. Collet   Single Speed

9.5 Amp/2 P

CRAFTSMAN

2 Peak HP

CRAFTSMAN

Chapter 1
ROUTER BASICS

If you've never used a router before or have routed only basic roundovers and grooves, you might have little idea of the range of cuts possible. But understanding the main functions of the router is sure to help you with your next project and every one thereafter, even if drawer joints and custom molding are a long way off. If you don't yet own a router, your first challenge will be choosing one from the long list of available models. Almost immediately, you'll start the process of acquiring bits and accessories, and to a greater extent, building jigs to make specific jobs easier—for routing is all about control, and a lot of your time will be spent devising ways to keep your router in line. The good thing is, once you make a path, the router will follow it every time with almost no variation.

An Introduction to Routing

Among workshop tools, the router is an undisputed king of versatility. There are few woodworking projects that can't be improved or made simpler by the router and its vast selection of bits. As an example, let's say that you'd like to build a coffee table. Using a router and a few ordinary bits, you can:

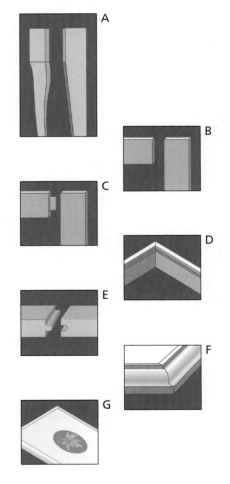

- Taper, shape, or surface the legs with custom details (A).
- Joint the frame pieces to a uniform width (B).
- Create mortise-and-tenon joints for assembling the frame (C).
- Rout a groove inside the frame for securing the tabletop (D).
- Build a glue-up top made with tongue-and-groove joints (or glue joints) (E).
- Square the edges of the top, then shape them with a decorative profile (F).
- And finally, just to impress your friends, add an inlay detail right in the center (G).

By building a simple coffee table you would learn all the router's primary functions: guide routing, edge-forming, joinery, and template routing. Following is an overview of these applications and the tools and gadgets available to make them easier.

Types of Routers & Bits

The two main types of routers for general workshop use are fixed-base and plunge. A third type, called a trim router, is a much smaller tool primarily used to trim plastic laminate (the countertop material).

Fixed-base routers are the standard-issue tools of the router family. They have a motor that's adjusted up or down on its base and is fixed in place for the routing operation. Standard fixed-base models range in power from 1½ to 2¼ horsepower and are suitable for most hand-held and table routing jobs. Large fixed-base tools, with 3 hp or more, are called heavy-duty, or production, routers and are used for heavy work with large bits. They also make excellent table routers.

Plunge routers have a special base that allows the motor to travel up and down while under power. This feature lets you plunge the spinning router bit down into the workpiece, move the tool sideways for a horizontal cut, then retract the bit from the wood at the end of the cut. Plunge routers can do everything standard fixed-base routers can do but are especially useful for inside cuts, such as mortises.

Trim routers, also called laminate trimmers, have small motors (1 hp or less) that are easy to grasp and control with one hand. They are convenient and effective for trimming laminate and for light edging work on wood and other materials. Like regular-size routers, trim routers make clean, accurate cuts, but their size limits them to small bits and shallow, light-duty work.

Router bits: While the router motor provides the muscle, the bit does all the cutting. With literally thousands of cutters to choose from, it's the bits that

A router and a selection of bits can produce many of the decorative and structural cuts for a project like this coffee table.

The plunge router (left) and fixed-base router (right) are the two main types of routers for general workshop use. A laminate router (center) is smaller and used primarily for trimming plastic laminate.

You can create your own router table, or purchase one. This is a small, easily portable benchtop table with an external switch and easy-access OFF button.

make routers the versatile tools they are. Most bits come with either a ¼"- or ½"-diameter shank, the solid shaft that is clamped to the router motor. Not all bits come in both shank sizes, so the smart shopper buys only routers that accept both (although trim routers accept ¼" only).

Table Routing

Hand-held routing is the standard method in which the router is held upright in your hands and is moved along the workpiece to make the cut. The alternative to this is table routing, where the router is inverted and attached to the underside of a flat table surface, with the bit protruding up through the table. The workpiece is slid along a vertical fence, where it contacts the bit to make the cut.

Most of the things you can do with hand-held routers can also be done on a table; in many cases, the table method is safer and more accurate. In general, tables are better for routing thin or narrow stock, which can't safely support the base of a hand-held router. Large bits are easier to control, and thus safer, in table-mounted routers, and the fence on a router table makes it good for milling and correcting flaws in stock.

A router table can be as simple as a thick MDF top with a hardwood stick clamped in place for a fence, although many woodworkers take it much further than that. There's also a full range of commercial tables available. Whatever is used, table routing is an aspect of routing that should not be overlooked, even by a beginner.

Routers make excellent dado cutters with the help of a straightedge guide.

Guide Routing & Edge-forming

Guide routing is a general term that covers basic hand-held routing cuts that are made with the help of a guide—a straightedge, a square, or a router edge guide, for example. Most guided cuts are made either parallel or perpendicular to the edge of a workpiece. One notable exception is routing circular cuts—something the router does better than any other tool. Typical guide-routing cuts include dadoes, grooves, squaring of stock, and decorative surfacing, such as fluting or beading.

Edge-forming is a type of guide routing that uses self-guided router bits—called piloted bits—to make controlled cuts. These bits have bearings attached at the end, middle, or top of the bit's cutter. The bearing rolls along a clean edge of the workpiece, or along a straight-edge or template, ensuring the bit cuts at a uniform depth. If you've ever used a router to round over the edges of a plywood panel or to shape the edges of a tabletop, you've done edge-forming. It's one of the router's signature functions, and there are more bits dedicated to edge-forming than to any other routing job.

Looking back to the sample coffee table project, guide-routing techniques can rout the grooves in the frame pieces and, with the help of a squaring guide, cut the tabletop to size with perfectly square edges. Edge-forming comes into play for routing the top's decorative finished edge.

A piloted ogee bit creates a uniform decorative edge on this tabletop.

Router Joinery

For most woodworkers, routers have replaced hand tools for joinery work. The accuracy and predictability of router cuts make them ideal for many different types of traditional joints: mortise-and-tenon, dovetail, box, and lap, to name a few. Even biscuit joints can be made with a router, for those who don't own a plate joiner. Complex joints, like cope-and-stick, lock-miter, and finger joints, can be made using specialty bits, although the bits can be pricey.

Most joinery cuts are made using hand-held routers and jigs or the router table. Some of the setups can be challenging, and, as with all joinery, there's a lot of trial and error. But once the setup is correct the actual routing techniques are easy. So, if you wanted to try out more joinery techniques on your coffee table, you could build custom drawers assembled with dovetail and drawer-lock joints.

With template routing, a flush-trimming, bearing-guided bit rides along a hardboard template to create the finished piece.

Routing with Templates

Cutting with templates is another job for which the router is the best tool available. As with joinery, there's much more work involved in setting up the cuts than in making them, but the results, again, are perfectly repeatable. Template routing uses a template, or pattern, secured above or below the work-piece. The router follows the template to cut a matching shape in the workpiece.

Commercially made templates are available for cutting hinge mortises and other precision work. You can make your own custom templates using a thin, flat material, like plywood, hardboard, or plastic. The router is fitted with a bearing-guided bit, so that the bearing rides along the template, or with a standard straight bit and a template guide. Using a flush-trimming bit or a pattern bit with a bearing that matches the cutter diameter produces a finished piece that is the same size as the template. When using a template guide (see page 126), the template must be smaller than the intended cut to allow for the offset between the guide and the cutting edges of the bit.

Guide bearing

Template guide

Template routing can accomplish an enormous range of tasks, including custom-shaping the legs on your coffee table, as well as creating the recess for the inlay. Because a shop-made template can take any form you like, template routing adds a great deal of creative potential to routing.

Building & Using Jigs

A jig is any kind of commercial or shop-made fixture that helps you make controlled and repeatable router cuts. A simple right-angle guide is a jig, and, in a sense, so is a router table. Most jigs are designed for a specific cut or project. You might make a jig for cutting a mortise or for holding a workpiece at an angle to make sloped cuts. Some jigs can be assembled in a few minutes; others are much more involved. The objective is always to make a particular routing task easier, faster, more accurate, and in many cases, safer.

A commercial jig for guiding a variety of mortise cuts, including hinge mortises.

Jig-making quickly becomes an obsession for most router users, and woodworking magazines are full of articles with ingenious shop-made jigs, revealing the hobby as somewhat of an art form. Your first jigs will be much simpler, of course, but the basic engineering concepts behind the simplest jig are often the same as those behind the most elaborate. Adapting the ideas to suit your own projects, tools, and work style is what jig-making is all about.

Choosing a Router

Routers are fairly basic tools but may have a lot of features, especially when compared to other portable shop equipment. Once you know what to look for, though, it's easy to pick over the different models in a given price range. Which brings up an important point: price. The common refrain from tool users is that you should always buy the best tool you can afford—better tools simply are more reliable, and their quality is reflected in the work they do. But the case for quality is particularly relevant to routers because the bits are so expensive.

Many manufacturers now make router kits that consist of a motor and both plunge (left) and fixed (right) bases.

If you're serious about routing, you'll soon have more invested in bits than in the router itself, so why run them in a cheap, underpowered tool?

Good routers are not inexpensive, but they are a good value. The majority of quality models fall into a mid-level price range, and any of them will likely be as much tool as you'll ever need. So, aside from price and features, the big decision you have to make is which type of router to buy. For general workshop routing the question is (or used to be) whether to go with a fixed-base or plunge router. Both can tackle most hand-held routing tasks, and both can be used in a router table—although pros and cons apply to each.

The following discussion outlines the features and benefits of both types. For those who can't decide, several major manufacturers now offer router kits that come with a motor and interchangeable fixed and plunge bases.

Most people buy a mid-size hand-held router for general use. If they end up logging a lot of hours on the router table or get into heavy production work, they look to a second, heavy-duty router with more horsepower. On the other end of the power scale, a trim router is a handy second tool for jobs that don't require much muscle.

Fixed-base Routers

Fixed-base routers are perfectly simple. From a user's standpoint, they have two main parts: the motor unit and the base. One distinct advantage of a fixed-base tool is that the motor slips or twists completely free of the base to facilitate bit changes or switching to a different type of base. The router is set up for action by securing the bit in the collet, which is fixed to the motor's shaft. The motor is inserted into the base, and the bit depth is adjusted by raising or lowering the motor position within the base, then it is locked in place using the base's clamping system. Attached to the bottom of the base is the subbase, a plastic disk with a center hole for the bit surrounded by a series of other holes for visibility. Most are opaque, but some routers have clear subbases for improved visibility.

Compared to plunge routers, the key drawback of the fixed-base tool is that the bit remains at one depth setting for each operation and cannot truly be plunged into the work as with a plunge router. "Plunging" with a fixed-base router involves setting one edge of the base on the workpiece so the bit spins freely, then slowly tipping the router to the horizontal while the spinning bit cuts into the wood at an angle. This is dangerous and difficult to do without ruining the cut.

Despite this disadvantage, many woodworkers prefer a fixed-base router for most hand-held routing work. With their lower center of gravity, handles that are close to the workpiece, and broad, round bases, fixed-base routers are inherently more stable than plunge types. This makes them better for edging, where less than 50% of the base surface is supported at all times. The simplicity and stability of fixed-base models also makes them easier to use with many types of jigs and templates. Finally, fixed-base routers are quite a bit cheaper than plunge routers, and their simpler designs make them less prone to maintenance problems.

When comparing fixed-base routers at the store, check for the following features:

Power: Mid-size fixed-base routers carry a power rating between 1½ and 2¼ hp. The higher the power rating, the more cabable the motor is of plowing through harder or denser material without slowing down.

Collet sizes: Most routers include both ¼" and ½" collets as standard equipment. Don't even consider a mid-size tool that accepts only ½" bits, as this will limit your bit choices considerably. Many manufacturers also offer ⅜" and metric collets as optional accessories, which can come in handy for special-size bits sometimes required for dovetail jigs and other setups. Some fixed-base routers require two wrenches for loosening and tightening collets.

Optional D-handle bases, or "pistol grips" are available for some routers.

Motor depth adjustment: There are a few different systems for adjusting the motor height: screw type, in which the motor housing has nubs that allow it to be spun into a threaded base; two-stage lever type with notches for coarse adjustments and a twist-knob for micro-adjustment; rack-and-pinion gear type; and motor ring type that engages threads ground into the motor housing. As long as the router is capable of very fine adjustment, the best system is a matter of personal preference.

Variable speed and soft start: Once a feature common only among production routers, electronic variable speed (EVS) now comes standard on many mid-size tools. This feature allows you to set the router's top speed at five or six different levels for specific routing situations. Electronic circuitry automatically maintains the motor speed through varying work loads and also helps absorb the shock of a sudden change in material (knots, etc.), giving you more control. Soft start brings the motor up to speed gradually and eliminates the kick you get when starting a standard router.

Base options: Some manufacturers offer a collection of bases for use with their fixed-base motors. Even if you don't buy extra bases initially, it's nice to have the optional accessories when your work calls for them. Specialty bases include a plunge base, for getting the best of both worlds with the same motor; a simplified fixed base to be used as a dedicated base for a router table; and a D-handle base, with a large pistol grip and trigger-style on/off switch. Some routers come with a D-handle base instead of a standard base with two knobs, but they cost more. Fans of D-handle bases believe they improve control; however, not everyone likes them, and they can be inconvenient with some setups, so try both types before deciding.

Usability features: Some features may affect the feel and convenience of the tool but are not necessarily deal-breakers. A great design feature for fixed-base routers is a motor cap with a flat top surface, allowing you to set the motor upside down on your bench for changing bits. Before buying any router, you should make sure you like the feel and positions of the handles. Weight may not be an important factor for everyone, but models in the mid-size range can vary by more than a pound. With bases and subbases, look for high visibility and large center holes made for big bits (although many brands offer various subbases as accessories).

Plunge routers move up and down on spring-loaded tubes, making them the ideal choice for stopped or blind cuts.

Plunge Routers

Plunge routers have been around since the 1950s but have only recently taken the limelight from fixed-base routers. They have motors that travel up and down on spring-loaded posts, or tubes, allowing precise, vertical plunging action of the bit to a preset depth. Bit depth is controlled by a depth stop that is set and locked in place before starting the router. At the end of the plunge stroke, the depth stop contacts the turret stop on the router's base. For multi-stage excavations, the turret stop can be rotated one step at a time to increase the bit depth incrementally with successive cuts.

Other design features include the plunge locking mechanism, which automatically locks the motor in place on the posts; flipping the lock lever is the last step before starting the cut. An up-stop feature limits the upwards travel of the motor so it stops at its original position. This can also be used to adjust bit depth when the router is in a router table. Many plunge routers have a spindle lock—a button that's depressed to hold the motor spindle in place while you loosen the collet with one wrench. Because plunge motors can't be removed from their bases, as fixed-base motors can, this feature simplifies bit changing.

As mentioned earlier, plunge routers can accomplish any task that a fixed-base tool can, but not always with the same ease and stability. The higher motor and handles and the relatively small (on many models), lightweight base of the plunge tool makes it more prone to tipping when the base isn't fully supported. Where plunge routers excel is making mortises and any other inside cuts that can't be accessed from the workpiece edge. Depending on the type of work you do, that can amount to a lot of cuts for which the plunge router is better suited.

Plunge routers naturally have several operating features that you should experiment with before making a decision. You'll also see a few bells and whistles offering this or that advantage. Here are the primary elements to check out:

Power: On average, plunge routers have a little more horsepower than fixed-base models. Most are 2 or 2¼ hp. The higher the power rating, the more capable the router and the less likely the router is to overheat and damage the motor.

Collets: Make sure the router accepts both ¼" and ½" collets. (See Collet sizes, page 14.)

Depth settings: The depth stop should be easy to adjust and have a clear, easy-to-read scale. Desirable additional features include a micro-adjust knob and a zero-out cursor. A multi-position turret stop is a must to make staged cuts without having to readjust.

Plunge depth and action: As the main reason you're buying a plunge router, the depth and smoothness of the plunge stroke are important features. Most models range between 2" and 2½" in plunge depth. Greater depth adds versatility. More importantly, the motor should always travel smoothly up and down on the plunge tubes.

Variable speed: Most plunge routers come with electronic variable speed (EVS) and soft start. (See Variable speed and soft start, page 14.)

Handles, plunge lock, and power switch: Ergonomics are important with plunge routers. Make sure the handles, plunge lock mechanism, and power switch fit your hands well and will be easy to operate under working conditions.

Other features: Scattered among the tool choices are some plunge router features that are helpful but not indispensable. An electric brake quickly stops the motor after it's switched off, helping to prevent accidents during deceleration. Vacuum chip collection can increase tool efficiency and bit life and improve workshop conditions. Some routers are designed for easy hookup to a vacuum system. Protective sleeves on plunge tubes are intended to prevent dust from fouling the plunge mechanism and can protect against dings from a slipped collet wrench. Since lateral stability is a general concern with plunge routers, you may prefer a model with a broad, round base over those with flat-sided bases.

Heavy-duty/ Production Routers

These routers, with standard 3 hp, 15-amp motors, are the Clydesdales of the router family. Most woodworkers buy these as second routers and use them for long runs and production work that would stress a mid-size machine. Heavy-duty routers also provide a lot of power for running large bits on the router table (see Router Table Routers, page 18). For hand-held work, big routers can tackle deep, single-pass cuts and large roundovers and are great for full-depth cuts in thick stock when template routing.

Heavy-duty routers are available as plunge and fixed-base, but few manufacturers offer models in both types. Electronic variable speed (EVS) and soft start are standard features for both types; the former is essential for large bits. Other features are the same as those commonly found on mid-size routers. Big routers perform

Long runs, large bits, and full-depth single-pass cuts require a heavy-duty router such as this model.

the same functions as mid-size tools, but their size and weight—between 12 and 15 pounds—make them relatively unwieldy and thus less desirable for general hand-held routing. If you do decide to go for the power, make sure the router you choose has a base (not the subbase) that can accommodate large-diameter bits.

ROUTER TABLE ROUTERS

What's the best type of router to use in a router table? The short answer is: a heavy-duty fixed-base model with variable speed. Now for the long answer: Almost any mid-size or heavy-duty fixed-base or plunge router will work, although some offer more convenience, power, and versatility than others. Here's a list of features to consider for good table routing:

• A 3 hp (15 amp) motor is nice if you want to do a lot of heavy work with big cutters or need to run the tool for long periods. Otherwise, a good, mid-size (10-12 amp) motor should suffice.

• Fixed-base routers are more convenient than plunge routers in tables because their motors can be removed from their bases for bit changes. Changing cutters with a plunge tool must be done from underneath the table, or you can mount the router's base to a mounting plate and pull the whole assembly from the table for changes. It's also more difficult to adjust bit depth on most plunge routers when they are inverted in a table—you're working against gravity as well as the plunge springs. A micro-adjust knob (often available as an accessory) helps considerably with plunge router adjustment.

• Variable speed, a base with a large opening, and a ½" collet are essential for running large bits, such as raised-panel cutters. A tool with a good bit depth range adds versatility.

Pull the entire mounting plate and router from the tabletop to change bits on a table-mounted plunge router.

Bit changing for table routing is easy with a fixed-base router because the motor can be removed from the base.

Trim Routers

Trim routers were designed for the precise but light-duty chore of trimming plastic laminate—a job that's usually done in cramped quarters or right on top of a counter, and where a mid-size router is too much tool and is more likely to scratch the finished surface. Everything about trimmers is geared toward this purpose: the small, usually round, motor casing fits into one hand so the other hand can hold the work; the high motor speed of around 30,000 rpm helps the bit cut quickly and cleanly; and a small base allows the tool to fit into tight spots.

All of these features make trimmers equally useful for light edge-forming, cutting shallow grooves, and template routing. Trim routers can't do most medium-duty routing tasks, and they can't use anything but the smallest standard router bits with ¼" shanks. As such, they're a good choice for a second-tool purchase if you already own a mid-size or bigger router. Trim routers are sold as part of a basic setup, including the tool and perhaps one or two base accessories, or as part of a complete trim kit, which includes the tool and three or more interchangeable bases designed for different trimming situations.

An offset base has an edge close to the bit for trimming in tight spaces or scribing a counter-top edge to a wall. Tilt bases can be set at 45 degrees for cutting bevels or working on angled surfaces. An underscribe base helps to cut perfectly matched edges for seaming laminate pieces. A trimmer edge guide is a handy accessory that comes standard with most trim routers. It has a bearing at the end of an adjustable arm that is mounted to the router's subbase, allowing you to make controlled flush-trimming and template cuts without using a bearing-guided bit, thus saving money on replacement bearings and eliminating the threat of a bearing seizing during use and marring the substrate surface.

When shopping for a trim router, compare:
• power ratings—most are between 4 and 6 amps
• bases and accessories
• ease of changing bases
• ease of adjustment
• weight and general ergonomics—the tool should fit comfortably in one hand

Power switch

Motor cap

Motor unit

Subbase

Router accessories include (from left to right) template guides, dovetail jigs, clear subbases, and various edge guides.

Router Accessories

Routers not only have more cutters than any other portabale power tool, they also have various accessories. Some, like extra collets and template adapters, come as standard equipment with new routers; others are optional products supplied by router manufacturers or aftermarket tool companies.

Subbases: Specialty subbases come in several shapes and sizes for both plunge and fixed-base routers. Common styles include clear bases for improved visibility, bases with large or small center holes to accommodate different bit diameters, and a stepped (underscribe) base for cutting seamed edges in plastic laminate. Offset subbases have a teardrop shape and a handle on the base to provide increased support and improved control of the router for edge work. A subbase-centering gauge, which comes standard with some routers, helps you set the subbase so it's perfectly concentric to the router's collet.

Edge guides: Edge guides connect directly to the router with steel rods fed through mounts in the router base. The guide's fence rides along the edge of the workpiece to make a variety of controlled cuts, including dadoes, grooves, and rabbets. Some edge guides also make circular and elliptical cuts (with additional accessories).

Templates & jigs: Commercial templates and jigs typically are high-grade metal fixtures manufactured to precise tolerances. Hinge-mortising templates, squaring guides, straightedges, and most commonly, dovetail jigs are available to help you make exact, repeatable cuts indefinitely without wearing out the jig.

Chip & dust collection: Routers are extremely messy. When the chips start flying, a collection system helps remove them from the cutting path and keep them out of the air. Some routers have vacuum ports built into their bases, handles, or plunge tubes, to which you attach a hose. For models that lack an integrated design there are accessories that mount to either top or bottom of the base, depending on the type of routing you're doing.

Maintaining Your Router

Most router maintenance problems occur in one of three areas: the collet, the base and height adjustment, and the motor's brushes. In general, the best thing you can do for your router is keep its parts clean. Eventually the motor bearings can wear out—indicated by rough travel or looseness of the shaft, excessive heat, and, at a more advanced stage, loud howling from the motor. You should have bad motor bearings replaced by a manufacturer's service center, but most other maintenance jobs can be done at home. See your owner's manual for service suggestions and instructions.

Clean & inspect the collet: As the only connection between the bit and router motor, the collet plays a critical role in the tool's performance, as well as its safety. Collets fouled by rust, dirt, resin, or abrasions don't hold bits tightly or on-center. To keep a collet in good condition, inspect it every time you install a bit. Leaving a bit in the collet when storing the tool can promote rust, so get into the habit of removing bits after use.

Clean a dirty collet with a non-abrasive cleaner and brush—never use sandpaper or emery cloth, which can remove metal and change the inner shape of the collet. Also clean the outer threads of the router shaft arbor and the tapered cavity inside the arbor. To clean the threads on the collet nut, remove the retaining ring on the end of the collet using snap-ring pliers. If it seems to need it, you can wipe

Remove the collet retaining ring with snap-ring pliers.

Once the collet retaining ring is removed, the collet can be screwed off the motor's spindle arbor.

a little light machine oil on the threads of the collet nut and arbor, but make sure there's no oil left on the inside of the collet, or its grip on the bit can be compromised.

Collets can also wear and fail to keep the bit in line while spinning, causing runout; or they can allow the bit to slip down in the middle of a cut. Any sign of slippage or excessive tool vibration is grounds for replacing the collet. One way to check for a worn collet is to load a straight bit into the collet and hand-tighten it. Move the bit back and forth from its end. If you detect any movement, replace the collet. Also replace a collet that shows any visible signs of damage or cracking along the edges. New collets are inexpensive and readily available through the router's manufacturer or a dealer. Most are self-contained and are installed by screwing right onto the router's spindle arbor.

Clean the motor & base: When a router motor moves begrudgingly up and down on its base and it gets harder and harder to make depth settings, it's time for a thorough cleaning. Start by blowing out the motor with compressed air (this is a good thing to do on a regular basis). For fixed-base routers, pull the motor from the base and clean the motor housing with a rag and perhaps a little machine oil, then polish it dry with a clean rag. Do the same to the inside wall of the base. If desired, you can add a thin coat of wax to the base to prevent sticking.

Plunge routers have more parts to clean and lubricate. If the plunge action is rough, release the motor from the plunge tubes and pull the springs from the tubes. Clean the tubes and springs, and use a rag or paper towel and a dowel to clean the plunge tube bores in the motor assembly. Clean any depth-setting parts you can reach.

Clean tubes on a plunge router by disassembling the base and using a dowel and a paper towel.

Replaceable brushes may be located under screw caps on either side of the motor.

You may need to remove the motor cap on some routers to access the brushes.

Before reassembling the router, lube the springs with lithium grease, and apply a little wax or dry lubricant to the plunge posts. Don't use grease or sticky lubricants on any exposed parts that can attract dust and chips.

Replace worn brushes: The universal-type motors that power all routers rely on two replaceable brushes to run. The brushes are small carbon blocks that rub against the motor's communicator to complete the electrical circuit that powers the motor. This contact slowly wears the brushes through attrition, and they typically should be replaced after 50 to 100 hours of running time. Since you probably aren't timing your router use with a stopwatch, it's a good practice to check the brushes once or twice a year. Replace them when they've worn to half their original length (most are ¾" long when new).

Letting the brushes wear too long can cause a few problems. The most obvious symptom is the motor cutting out during use or failing to start at all. Before that happens, you might notice more than usual sparking from under the motor cap. Neglecting worn brushes can cause damage to the communicator and possibly jeopardize the life of the motor.

Checking and replacing brushes is easy. They may be located behind two large screw caps at either side of the motor, or you may have to remove the plastic motor cap and peer down to find the brushes. If you can't find them, check the parts diagram in your owner's manual. Carefully remove the screw cap (there may be a spring assembly attached to the brush) or pull back the spring holding the brush in place and pull out the brush. If either brush is worn halfway or more, buy two new ones from the manufacturer. Always replace both brushes at the same time.

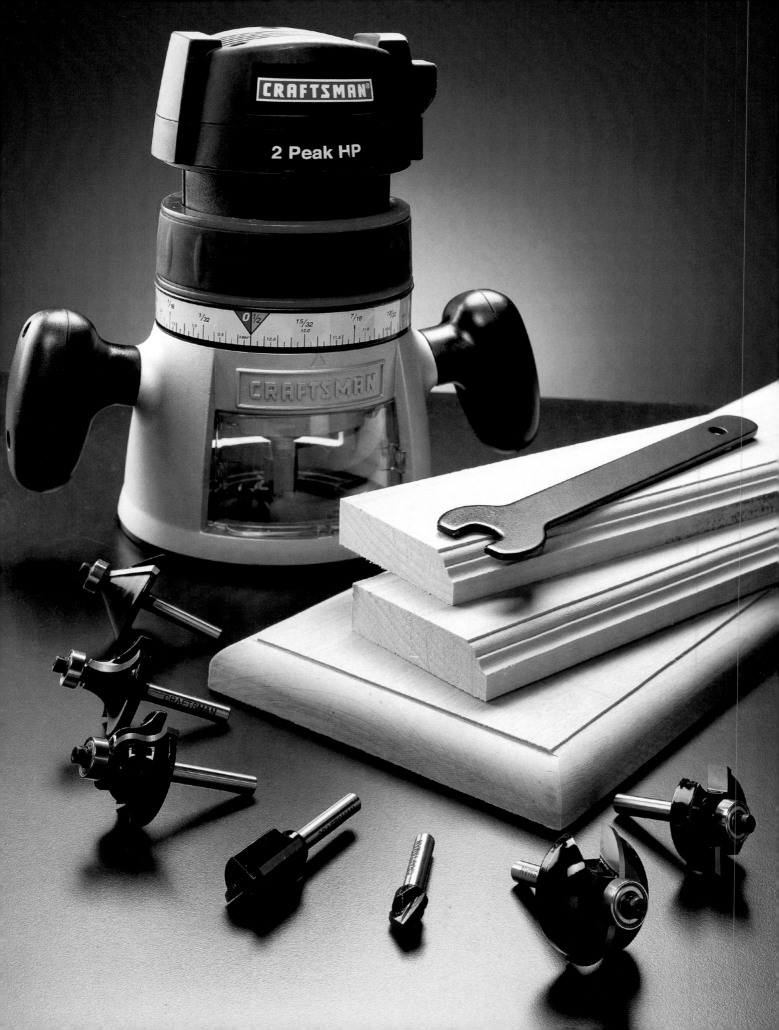

Chapter 2
ROUTER BITS

Before building a jig or devising a setup for any project, you'll need to decide on the best bit for the job. Over time you'll find that acquiring bits is one of the more appealing aspects of routing. Inevitably, it's also the most expensive. Even a basic collection of quality carbide bits can easily cost more than a standard router. What's important to remember is that all routers are little more than fancy motors without bits to do their cutting. Therefore, to get the most from your router, you must do three things: buy good bits, take good care of them, and always use an appropriate bit for each job.

Router bits are highly engineered tools for good reason. At a standard router speed of 24,000 rpm, a two-flute bit makes 800 cuts per second. With all the forces at work, making a clean cut requires a tool designed for balance, cutting efficiency, and rigidity. Bits are primarily categorized by the type of cut they make. Other important criteria include material, shank diameter, flute number and style, and overall size.

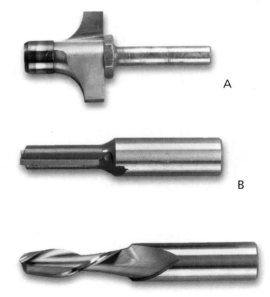

Bit Materials
Most router bits fall into one of three material categories: high-speed steel (HHS), carbide-tipped, and solid-carbide. For most routing tasks, carbide-tipped bits offer the best balance of quality and price, as you'll see.

High-speed steel (HSS): These bits have steel cutting edges and, for the most part, are economy-grade. Steel cutters can actually be made sharper than carbide, but they dull much faster, offering only 10% to 20% the service life of a carbide edge on average. Some woodworkers prefer steel bits for specific tasks, such as plunging cuts, but these people also tend to do their own bit sharpening. For most router users, a steel bit is good only for short-run jobs, and will be thrown away before long.

High-speed steel roundover bit with integral pilot (A), carbide-tipped straight bit (B), and a solid-carbide spiral bit (C).

Carbide-tipped bits: By far the most common and widely used bits are carbide tipped. Their bodies are made of steel with brazed-on carbide cutting edges. These bits are more expensive than HSS but last 5 to 10 times longer, because a quality carbide-tipped bit can be professionally sharpened between four and six times before the edges are gone. Carbide is tough enough to perform well with a variety of materials, including plywood and other manufactured sheet goods, which are hard on cutter edges.

Solid-carbide bits: These are a step up in quality from carbide-tipped bits and are, naturally, more expensive. Solid-carbide is available in a limited range of bit styles, primarily those for simple functions, such as flush-trimming, grooving, beveling, and boring. It's also used for high-quality spiral bits, which offer the smoothest cuts and unmatched efficiency for trimming and plunge cuts.

Bit Anatomy

Knowing a little about the basic design elements of router bits will help you select the proper bits and give you points to compare when shopping. All router bits have a shank, which is chucked into the router collet; a body; and cutters (although some bits have only one). The flutes are the cutaway spaces in front of the cutters. Flutes are sometimes called gullets or chip pockets because they provide a space for catching and ejecting the waste chips removed by the cutters. Bits that are piloted, or bearing-guided, have a ball-bearing pilot attached to the shank that controls the bit's cutting depth, although some pilots come in the form of a small, solid pin on the end of the bit or a smooth section of the shank that serves as the pilot.

The photo at left shows the basic elements of a router bit and some of the terms commonly used for bit specification. Note that the "usable length" of the shank includes only the completely cylindrical portion. The area where the shank cuts away into the flute (or where it flares out as it meets the bit body) should not be placed into the collet and therefore doesn't count as usable length. This dimension typically is not provided by the manufacturer, so you'll have to measure it yourself when choosing a bit.

Overall diameter is an important consideration for several reasons. First, the bit must be smaller than the center hole in your router's subbase. If it's too big, you'll have to find or make an alternative subbase. Second, large-diameter bits are safer and more effective at slower speeds—as a general rule, bits over 1¼" in diameter should run at less than 18,000 rpm. You need a variable-speed router to use these bits properly. Bits over 1¼" in diameter are often tricky to use and typically should be used only on a router table.

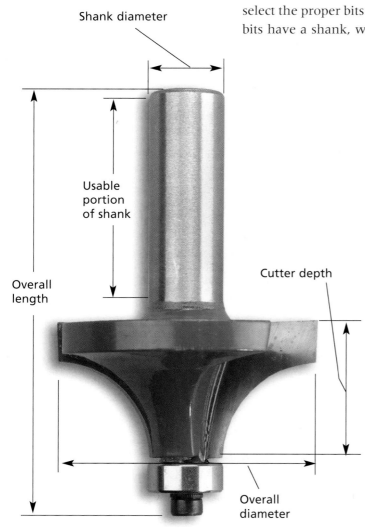

Shank diameter

Usable portion of shank

Overall length

Cutter depth

Overall diameter

When purchasing router bits, you will see specifications including the diameter, shank size, and height or cutter depth. For some roundover bits, the radius of the rounded section also may be given.

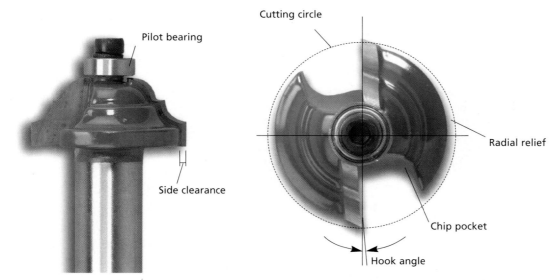

Other router bit features include the number of flutes and cutters, rake angle, side clearance, and pilot bearings.

Bit Geometry

A bit's geometry refers to the design features of the body and cutters, all of which directly affect the bit's performance. While the effects of the geometry may be not be obvious, over time you'll probably develop preferences for certain features.

Number of flutes: The flute and cutter number is always the same. Two-flute bits are by far the most common and typically offer the most effective balance of efficiency and quality of cut. Also common are one-flute bits, which are designed for quick chip ejection and higher feed rates but which don't always cut as cleanly as two-flute styles. Three-flute and four-flute bits are available in some styles. While additional flutes can produce a cleaner cut, it's often at the cost of reduced body stiffness and limited waste clearance.

Shear angle: The position of the cutting edges is the shear angle. They may be set vertically (called straight flute) or at a slight angle (called shear or on-shear bits). Shear cutters are more efficient because they meet the wood at an angle, creating a slicing motion in contrast to the chopping effect of a straight cutter. The greater efficiency produces smoother cuts and requires less power from the router. Shear cutters typically are available only on bits of ¾" or greater diameter, and they appear on many decorative bits. Given the choice, most woodworkers prefer shear bits over straight.

Rake or hook angle: The cutter's angle relative to the center of the bit is the rake or hook, and thus the angle at which the edge contacts the wood. A greater rake angle yields a smoother cut and allows for faster feed rates.

Side clearance: Side clearance is the difference between the bit's cutting diameter and the diameter of the solid part of the body. On a spinning bit, this clearance provides a space for waste and reduces friction.

Radial relief: This refers to the design of the cutter's back side, which is "relieved" to reduce friction. A radiused, or rounded, relief is better than a flat relief because it places greater supporting mass behind the cutting edge. This support helps the cutter hold an edge longer, reduces chipping, and aids in resharpening.

THE ANTI-KICKBACK FEATURE

Kickback on a router occurs when a bit initially engages the wood and takes too large a bite for the tool to handle, forcing the router (or the work) backward, opposite the feed direction. This is more likely to happen when using a standard router bit without an anti-kickback design. The anti-kickback feature uses increased body mass (often in the form of "wings" that extend into the flute) to limit the cutting depth possible with each revolution of the bit. In many cases, the extra body mass not only prevents kickback but also gives the bit greater balance and stability. The feature is not essential for safe routing, but given the advantages, it makes sense to buy bits that have the feature if they're available.

The bit on the right has anti-kickback wings.

Shopping for Bits

While the overall selection of router bits is staggering, shopping for the right bit is not a complicated task. The best approach is to decide which features you need—for your router and the type of work you'll be doing—and to shop for a good value using those criteria.

Price alone is not the only indicator of quality, but it's one of the best. Unless you want to try out a new profile or you have a one-time, quickie job to do, ignore the cheapest range of bits. This typically includes most high-speed steel bits and even low-grade carbide-tipped bits. Cheap bits may perform adequately at first, but they dull and otherwise wear so quickly that they'll cost you more in the long run. At the other end of the spectrum are bits that exceed the demands and budget of the part-time woodworker. For beginners up through serious hobbyists, better-quality carbide-tipped bits are the best choice.

If you've never bought bits before, a good place to start is with a well-established manufacturer that has a good reputation for their tools or cutter products. A few of the good router manufacturers make quality bits, but most come from tooling companies that may also make saw blades and drill bits. Catalogs from bit manufacturers are great resources—looking over the various profiles and bit choices can inspire new ideas and help you plan projects. They also give you the critical specifications for each bit. Good resources for information are woodworking journals, which occasionally publish reviews of bit manufacturers.

Regardless of how or where bits are bought, the best assessment of their quality happens at home. Close visual inspections—of the bit and the cut it makes—and using the bit for a while will help you decide whether to buy from the same manufacturer again. It's a good idea to start with one or two bits to see if you like them before investing a lot in one brand.

The features listed below will help you find the best bits for performance, longevity, and safety. Also included are some of the details typical for better-quality bits—not all of the features are must-haves for every bit, but it helps to know what you're paying for.

Shank diameter: Router bit shanks are commonly available with ¼" and ½" diameters, and less commonly with ⅜". As a general rule, ½" shanks are better than ¼", for several reasons. A larger shank is stiffer and stronger, making it more resistant to vibration, deflection, and breakage. A greater surface area means that the collet gets a better grip on the shank. A larger bit also transmits less heat from the motor to the cutter. As a clincher, ½" bits often cost about the same as their ¼" counterparts. When prices do vary, it's usually not enough to warrant getting the smaller shank size. Bits with small cutters typically have ¼" shanks, and that's fine; heavier shanks are needed more for large cutters that do heavy-duty work.

Shank length: The usable portion of a bit's shank should be long enough to extend at least ¾" into the collet, so that the bit is held securely and won't vibrate or deflect. Make sure the shank has a little extra length if you want it to receive a shank bearing. To prevent damage to the collet and provide easy insertion, a shank should be smoothly chamfered or beveled at its top end. A rough or sharp edge can easily damage a collet. The shank's finish should be perfectly clean and smooth.

Cutter quality: A bit's cutting edges can reveal a lot about its quality, and they directly affect its performance and longevity. Assuming that you're looking for carbide-tipped bits, be aware that not all carbide is equal. Better bits are made with micrograin carbide, which wears slower and cuts cleaner than coarse-grain carbide and can be sharpened more times.

While it's not always easy to determine the type of carbide, there are a few obvious things you can look for. Check each cutter's grind by running your fingernail along the front and back edges. They should be smooth and flat. Also compare the thickness of the carbide cutters with those of other brands—thicker is better. Finally, make sure the weld between the carbide and bit body is complete (without voids) and there are no burrs or inconsistencies.

Cutter length: In contrast to shank diameter, bigger is not necessarily better with regard to the cutter length. In fact, the longer the cutter, the more prone a bit is to deflection and vibration. Longer cutters can also require thicker jigs or templates to work effectively. So, for a given procedure or setup, a shorter cutter that can do the job effectively is the better choice.

Body construction: Make sure the bit's body has smooth surfaces and a clean finish. Roughness and poor design lead to resin buildup and inefficient waste clearance.

Paint & other coatings: Many bits these days have painted bodies or are treated with a non-stick coating. The smooth coatings help reduce friction and resin buildup and are intended to speed waste ejection. Bright, candy-like paint colors have undeniable appeal, and they can also improve visibility of the bit during use. The paint also helps prevent corrosion.

Bits to avoid: Poorly engineered bits can be vulnerable to breakage during use—a scary thought at 20,000-plus rpm. Here are some bit characteristics to look out for: bits with ¼" shanks and large cutters; unusually long, thin straight bits; dovetail bits with very narrow necks; and very thin grooving bits. As a general rule, select a ½" shank for any bearing-guided bit. The sideways (deflection) stress placed on piloted bits during use can be too great for ¼"-shank bits.

Types of Bits

There's really no science or method for classifying the hundreds of different types of router bits. Here they are grouped primarily by the type of work they do, which in turn dictates certain design characteristics—for example, most grooving bits have plunge-cut capabilities, while edge-forming bits are usually piloted. A manufacturer's catalog may arrange their bits quite differently.

Grooving & surfacing bits: The primary grooving tool, and perhaps the single most-useful, is the straight bit. This has both side- and bottom-cutting capability and is effective for cutting dadoes, rabbets, mortises, and tenons, and for trimming, bottom-cleaning, and general stock removal. A straight bit with a guide bearing mounted to its shank is called a pattern bit and is used for template routing and straightedge-guided work. Straight bits cover a broad range of sizes, styles, and capabilities. One specialty type is the plywood dadoing bit (commonly available in sets), which is sized slightly small to match the actual thickness of plywood.

There's also a great variety of decorative grooving bits, used for everything from cutting reeds and flutes into the surface of stock to freehand carving and sign-making. Some of the most popular decorative grooving bits include: core-box, V-groove, veining, and point-cutting and other decorative bits that plunge vertically into the work, then cut a decorative profile horizontally.

Surfacing bits have relatively wide, short bodies that make side cuts and flat, smooth bottom cuts. This category includes mortising bits, which cut shallow recesses for door hinges; dishing bits, used for carving out wide areas, such as on wooden trays and seat bottoms; and dado planer bits, which cut wide, flat-bottomed dadoes and can be used for surfacing stock. Smoothing or leveling rough stock, stripping paint, and limited amounts of planing can be done using a router with a wide, flat-bottoming bit and a jig built for the purpose. Many surfacing bits have shank-mounted bearings for use with a template.

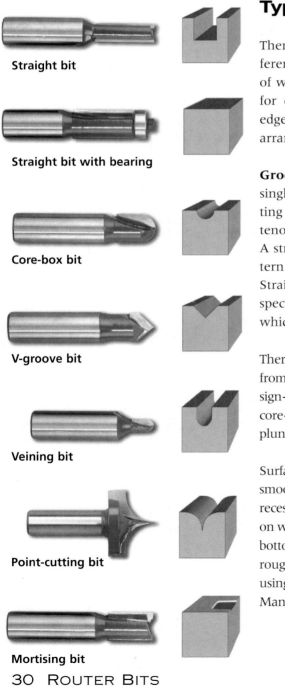

Straight bit

Straight bit with bearing

Core-box bit

V-groove bit

Veining bit

Point-cutting bit

Mortising bit

Edge-forming bits: Edge-forming bits cut decorative profiles into the edges of stock and, in the case of custom molding, into the faces of narrow trim material. Edge-forming is probably the most common type of routing and involves the greatest variety of bit types. Most edge-forming bits are piloted and have an attached bearing that rolls along the workpiece, template, or guide so that the bit cuts at a uniform depth. Bargain bits often have a solid piloting pin that spins along with the rest of the bit. Solid pilots have a tendency to burn or scar the workpiece as they move along the edge and for this reason should be avoided. Most edge-forming bits have bearings at the end of the bit, and in some cases the bearings can be changed to alter the bit's cutting depth (see Bit bearings, page 33).

The decorative profiles on edge-forming bits allow you to cut everything from a simple roundover or chamfer to traditional classical details, such as ogee, cavetto, and cove and bead. Rabbeting bits, which are also piloted, make right-angle cutouts into stock edges for joinery or for letting in glass or panels into wood frames. You can use any combination of edge-forming bits to mill custom molding. Some manufacturers offer a multi-form, or multi-profile, bit designed to cut a wide range of molding details using various setups.

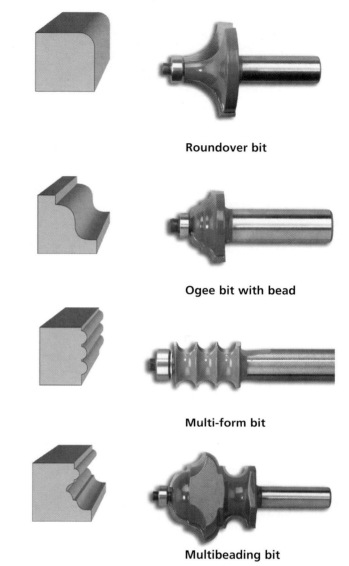

Roundover bit

Ogee bit with bead

Multi-form bit

Multibeading bit

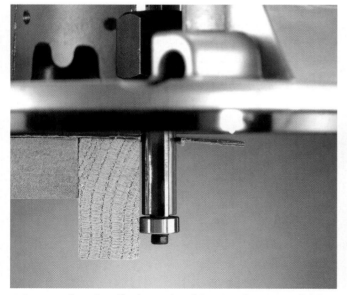

A bottom-bearing flush-cutting bit trims laminate flush to the substrate.

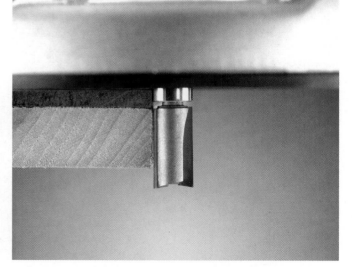

A flush-trimming pattern bit cuts stock (below) flush with the template (above).

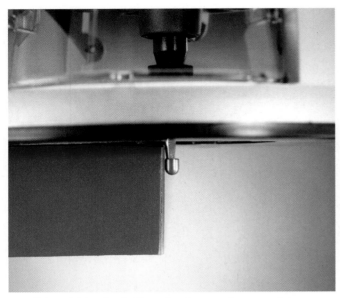

A solid-carbide single-flute laminate trimmer with a beveled edge trims laminates perfectly.

A removable shaft-mounted bearing is held in place by a stop collar with setscrew.

Some guided bits come with a variety of bearings of different sizes to change cutting depth.

Trimming bits: Trimming bits, or flush-trim bits, are straight bits that are piloted either by a bearing or by the bit's shank. The classic style is a two-flute bit with the bearing mounted at the tip. The bearing has the same diameter as the cutter; it rides along a template or substrate, and the bit trims flush any overhanging material. Trimmers with shank pilots are not the same as the cheap edge-forming bits with piloting pins. They typically are solid-carbide, one-flute bits designed for trimming plastic laminate. While both bearing- and shank-piloted bits are good for trimming laminate, some professionals prefer shank pilots, because they eliminate the risk of a bearing seizing and burning the laminate substrate.

A pattern bit is a straight bit with a bearing mounted to the shank above the cutter. This is used with a template or straightedge to make flush-trim cuts (if the bearing matches the cutter diameter) or, if the bearing is larger than the cutter, to make cuts where the cut is offset from the template.

Because deflection is an issue, particularly with bottom-bearing trimming bits, choose the shortest, stoutest bit practical for the job. Avoid long, narrow trimming bits, and always trim using a minimum of sideways pressure on the bearing.

Bit Bearings

Bearing-guided bits use a simple system to produce reliable, accurate cuts: the bit can cut only as deep as the bearing will allow. With many types of bearing-guided bits, you can change the bearing to get different cuts. For example, a 1"-diameter rabbeting bit with ½"-diameter bearing will cut a ¼"-wide rabbet. Switching to a ⅜" bearing allows for a ⁵⁄₁₆"-wide rabbet.

Bearings can also be added to standard bits, using a stop collar secured with a setscrew to hold the bearing on the bit's shank. This can turn a straight or spiral bit into a pattern bit that can be used for template routing. When using stop collars, make sure the setscrew doesn't project beyond the outer edge of the bearing and interfere with the bearing's travel. If the factory setscrew is too long, replace it with one from a hardware store.

It's important to inspect bearings for wear before each use. Run the bearing along your hand—if you feel any roughness in its travel, don't use it. At the extreme operating speeds of routers, bearings are highly stressed and can seize suddenly, resulting in a burned or scored workpiece. Bearings can also blow apart. Replacement bearings are available for ¼" and ½" bit shanks in a variety of outer diameters. Buying them from bit manufacturers ensures that the bearings are the right size and are designed for the rigorous conditions of routing. It's also a good idea to have some extra bearings for your most-used bits, so your work is not interrupted by bad bearings.

Joinery bits: Cuts for many types of joinery are routed using basic bits, such as straight, rabbeting, mortising, and dado bits. Dovetail bits are made specifically for cutting dovetails joints. Specifications for dovetail bits include cutting diameter, cutting height, and the degree of angle at which the cutters are set .

Other joints are made possible with special joinery bits. Popular types include lock-miter, glue-joint, finger-joint, rail-and-stile (cope-and-stick), tongue-and-groove, window sash, biscuit cutter, and drawer-lock bits. These bits are commonly available in one-piece designs, which require changes to the setup and sometimes the bit to cut both sides of the joint; and in two-piece sets, which require one setup change but are generally more convenient and accurate than their one-piece counterparts.

Spiral bits: Spiral bits have one or more cutting edges that spiral up their shank somewhat like a drill bit. This creates a continuous cutting action that produces exceptionally clean cuts with little tearout and reduced stress on the router motor. Used primarily as alternatives to standard straight bits, spirals are made with high-speed steel or solid carbide.

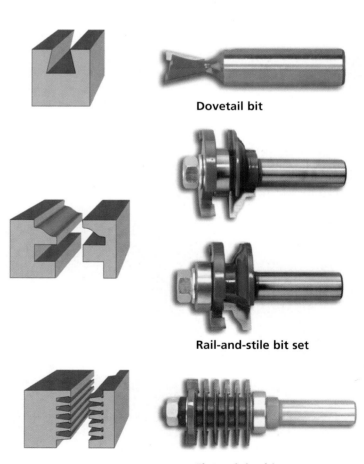

Dovetail bit

Rail-and-stile bit set

Finger-joint bit

An up-cutting spiral bit leaves fuzz on the top surface of the cut material.

A down-cutting spiral bit leaves fuzz on the bottom surface of the cut material.

A compression bit, which consists of both up- and down-cutting spirals, leaves a clean edge on both surfaces.

In addition to clean cuts, spiral bits are great for plunge-cutting, since they go in like drill bits, making them effective for deep blind mortises and through mortises. The spiraled flutes pull chips out and away from the cutting path better than any other type of bit. Up-cut spirals eject waste upwards, making them the better choice for deep grooves and mortises; down-cut spirals send chips down and are preferred for through mortises and cutting dados or grooves into faces where a clean top edge is desired. Both types leave a light fuzz of splinters on the exit face of the wood. Compression spirals have up-cutting flutes on the lower portion of the bit and down-cutting flutes on the upper portion—perfect for trimming stock with surface veneers on both sides.

Spirals are more efficient that straight bits and stay sharper much longer, but they do have some drawbacks. First, a solid-carbide two-flute spiral bit can cost more than twice what a carbide-tipped straight bit costs. It's also more difficult to find a shop that can sharpen spirals. Because of their design, spiral bits can be tricky to use. Down-cut spirals can force the router upward and test your grip on the tool, while up-cut bits want to pull up the workpiece, so like all cuts, it must be clamped securely.

Specialty bits: Being the most versatile portable tool in the workshop, it's not surprising that the router can accommodate a host of specialty bits for all kinds of professional and home-improvement jobs. Here's a sampling of some out-of-the-ordinary but readily available bits:

Keyhole bits create slots for hanging plaques, mirrors, shelf brackets, etc. A larger plunging section at the tip of the bit bores the entry hole and a narrower upper section routs the slot.

Keyhole bit

Burr bits have diamond-cut bodies and are used for routing fiberglass, epoxy, and other non-metallic composite materials.

Burr bit

Raised-panel bits cut the tapered edges for making traditional raised panels. These are often used with rail-and-stile bits to create raised-panel doors.

Chipbreaker bits allow for high feed rates on abrasive materials such as plywood, particleboard, chipboard, and non-ferrous metals. Their special design breaks up the chips during cutting and helps the bits last much longer than standard bits.

Raised-panel bit

Bowl-beveling bits can cut round-sided recesses in wood stock.

Inlay kits include a small down-spiral bit, a template guide, and a bushing. Using a template, you cut out the recess in the workpiece, then remove the bushing from the guide to cut the inlay to size.

Chipbreaker bit

Multi-piece bits have an arbor end that holds a variety of different cutters or replaceable blades.

Bowl-beveling bit

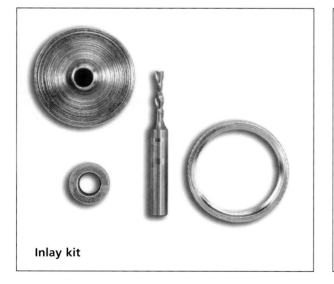

Inlay kit

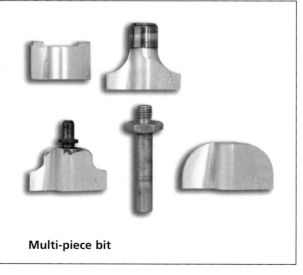

Multi-piece bit

Resin on this bit increases friction, which causes excess heat buildup.

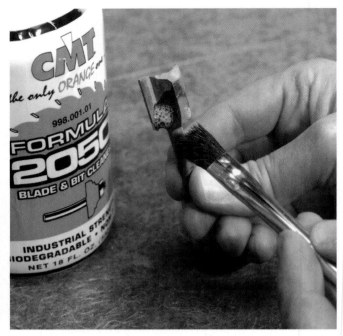

Clean regularly with bit cleaner and a nylon brush to maintain peak bit efficiency.

Maintaining Your Bits

Keeping router bits clean and sharp is just as important as using quality bits. Sharpening your own carbide is simply too difficult to be practical, and it's a good way to distort the cutting edges or destroy the balance of the bit. Some people like to touch up carbide bits between professional regrindings, but proper care and thoughtful use of your bits will get you just as far. The brittle edges of carbide bits can chip fairly easily when knocked against metal tools or other carbide edges. A simple storage system will keep your bits safe and close at hand.

Cleaning bits: Dirty bits, like dull ones, make poor cuts. Buildup of pitch, resins, and dust on bits creates added friction to the cutting action and hinders chip ejection. More friction means more heat and prematurely dull edges. It's a good practice to clean bits after each use, so they're ready to go next time. If necessary, clean bits as needed during a job, especially if you're cutting resinous softwoods.

Cleaning is easy: Spray the bit's body and cutters with a commercial router bit cleaner (available at woodworking stores), wait a few minutes, then brush the parts with a nylon or soft brass brush. Wipe down the bit and inspect the shank to make sure it's clean and smooth with no scratches or burrs that could damage a collet (see Maintaining Your Router, page 21, for more information on collet care).

Never use a metal tool, such as a knife or screwdriver, to clean a bit. You'll scratch the body's smooth passages or chip or score the carbide edges. If your bits tend to rust a little while in storage, apply a dry lubricant made for router bits after cleaning. Clean pilot bearings carefully and inspect them for wear by spinning them with your hand. Do not soak bearings in solvent, which can dissolve their internal lubrication.

Carbide is brittle and easily damaged. Storing bits in a drilled board will increase their life expectancy.

Storing Bits

Whether you keep them tucked away in custom-made drawers or just set them on a shelf, the simplest and most effective way to store router bits is to place them shank-down into holes drilled into a board. This keeps the cutter edges away from one another and gives you a good view of the profiles for easy bit selection. The worst thing you can do is toss your bits into a drawer or toolbox, where their edges will dull one another or they'll become chipped by other tools dropped into the drawer.

Make a storage board from 1½" (2×) stock or two layers of ¾" plywood. Drill a series of holes sized for the shanks of your bits—¹⁷⁄₆₄" holes for ¼" bits; ³³⁄₆₄" holes for ½" bits. Spacing the holes about 1½" apart works well for most bits; just make sure the bits won't touch and that you'll have enough room to grab each one without endangering your fingers. For a large bit collection, you might want to build a simple shelving system with a box carcase and dadoed sides, where the storage boards double as pull-out shelves.

A worn or nicked blade will result in burned areas or a flawed cut.

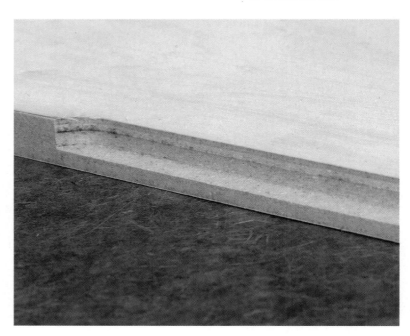

Identifying a dull bit: Dull router bits send clear signals to let you know when it's time to resharpen. Usually the first indication is that it's harder than normal to feed the router or workpiece, and there will be a noticeable increase in the motor's noise. Several clues may be found in the cut. A dull bit can burn the wood or leave a bumpy or otherwise flawed cut. Waste removed by a dull bit often

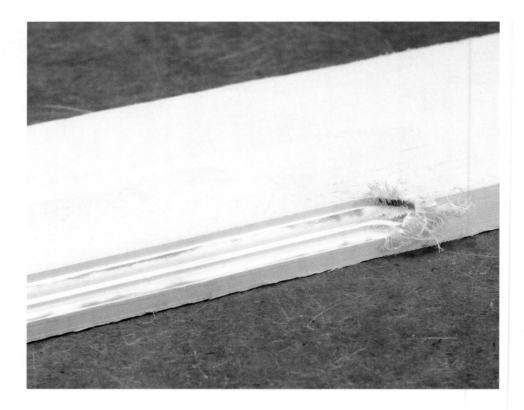

Burning and torn, rather than cut, fibers indicate a worn bit.

looks more like sawdust than sliced shavings. On softwood, dull bits will tear the fibers from the wood rather than slice them. Because bits often get used more in one capacity than another, it's typical for them to wear unevenly along the length of their cutters. One sign of this kind of wear is a line or step that appears on a workpiece when the bit is set deeper than it usually is. You can check for this by making a test cut with the bit set at full depth.

Also take a look at the bit itself: Shiny, burnished areas along a cutting edge indicate dullness. Chipped carbide is an obvious cry for help. Regrinding can eliminate shallow chips, but a severely chipped bit should be thrown out.

A dull bit will often have shiny, burnished areas.

Sharpening bits: For serious router users, a good sharpening service is a valuable resource. A well-made carbide-tipped bit can be sharpened four or more times in its life. Depending on your usage, you may never have to sharpen most of your bits. If you do, be aware that even a proper grinding can change the size or geometry of a bit. When the size or angle of the cutting path is critical, such as with flush-trimming bits and those used for joinery, you're taking a risk by having them sharpened. Edge-forming bits and straight bits used for basic material removal generally can be sharpened without creating problems.

In any case, it's important to find a service that knows router bits. A shop that does saw blades and other carbide tooling is more likely to do quality work than a standard knife-and-scissors service. Those with specialty services might sharpen spiral bits, re-tip carbide bits, and grind custom bits. If you can't find someone locally, check with your favorite router bit manufacturer (some offer sharpening services), as well as mail-order services advertised on-line and in woodworking magazines. Before trusting a shop with your favorite or most expensive bits, bring in a couple of standard bits for test sharpening.

To inspect the quality of a sharpening, use a magnifying glass and some test cuts. Under the glass, the bit's cutting edges should have a smooth finish with no chips, which would indicate grinding that was too coarse. Make sure the edges have not been ground excessively—removing too much carbide unnecessarily shortens the bit's life. A poor sharpening effort may show up on the workpiece, too. If tiny chips appear on the cutter edges after brief use, the bit may have been overheated during sharpening. Also, if the bit vibrates more than it used to, the grinding was not balanced and should be redone.

High-speed steel bits can be sharpened with standard sharpening stones. Carbide bits require special stones and extra care when sharpening.

Extending bit life. Using your router bits will make them dull; however, you can extend their lives and the time between sharpening. As a general practice, complete cuts incrementally, making light (about ⅛"-deep) cuts with each pass. Some bits, like dovetails, must be cut at full depth in one pass, but you can reduce wear on these bits by making an initial pass with a narrow straight bit to remove the bulk of the material.

Old bits that are too dull to cut cleanly can be used to make the majority of a cut, leaving a final light pass for a newer, sharper bit. If a bit is worn near its tip—a common occurrence—try a setup that utilizes the less-used part of the cutters. For example, a bearing-guided chamfer bit, when used in a hand-held router, will always cut from the portion closest to the bearing. Using the same bit in a router table and positioning the fence past the bearing plane lets you cut anywhere along the bit's edges. When trimming plywood edges with a straight bit, periodically move the bit up or down slightly to avoid uneven wear caused by the glue lines between plies. The glue is more abrasive than the wood and will dull (or even chip) the carbide more quickly.

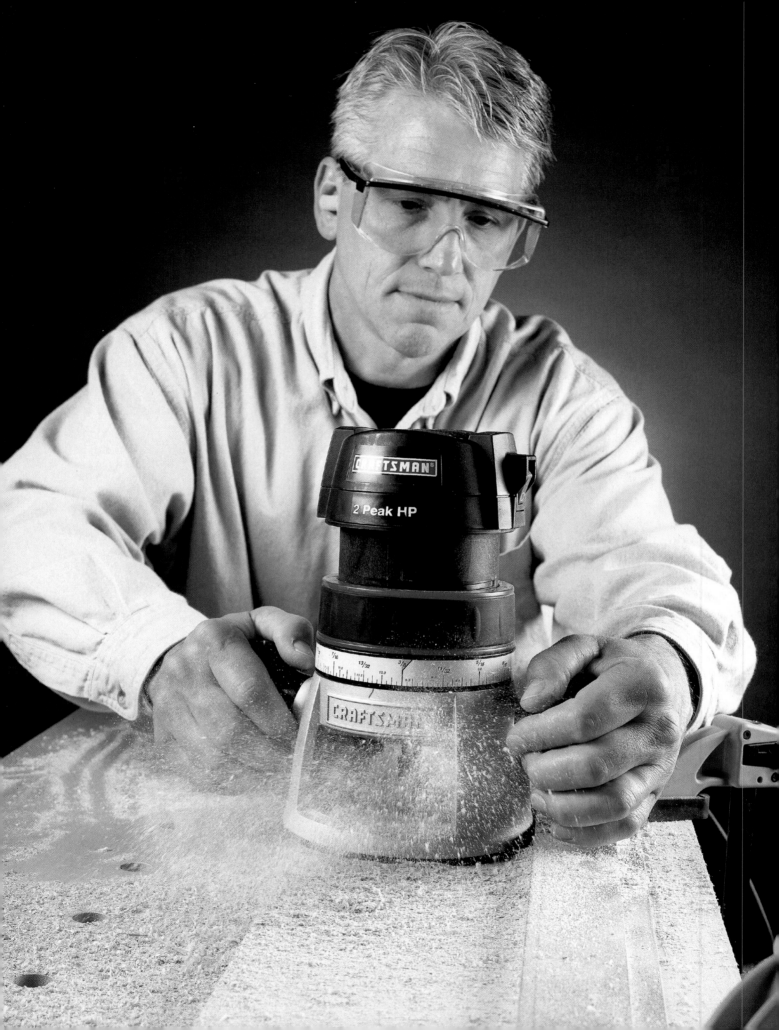

Chapter 3
GETTING STARTED

Good routing technique starts with a few sound work habits. As alsways with any piece of equipment, read the owner's manual thoroughly, and keep it handy for reference. Each job should begin with a simple process of 1) carefully setting up the cut, 2) making a quick safety check, and 3) running test cuts to ensure accuracy. It's the same systematic approach used by expert woodworkers and is the best way to avoid mistakes. This chapter covers the essentials of hand-held routing—things you'll need to know before getting to work. Much of the information given here, including material preparation, general safety, and understanding cutting depth and feeding methods, also applies to table routing. However, several additional techniques and safety issues peculiar to the router table are covered in Chapter 4.

Router Safety

Safe routing goes hand-in-hand with quality cuts: the better you set up the cut, the more controlled the router will be—and a controlled cut is a safer cut. This relationship is a fortunate one for home-shop woodworkers, many of whom would sooner risk their own skin than an expensive piece of hardwood. In addition to the setup there are safety considerations regarding what you should wear when routing, tool maintenance, and of course, operating the router.

Safe setup: With a thoughtful setup and a few quick checks before powering up, you'll greatly reduce the chances of ruining a workpiece, breaking a bit, or losing control of the tool. Always clamp your work securely. A workpiece slipping or falling over in the middle of a cut will not only spoil the cut but can break the bit. Supporting the router's base adequately should be the first requirement for any jig or setup. It's also important to use clean, straight, and square stock. Poorly milled material can behave unpredictably when you machine it.

Safety gear: The router is one of the loudest tools in the shop. If you run one without ear protection, hearing loss is merely a matter of time. As for your eyes, much of routing is done with your face fairly close to the spinning bit. Never remove the manufacturer's chip shield. and always wear safety glasses. Among the common hazards of routing are flying pieces of knots, carbide chips from a bit's cutting edge, and a broken-bit-turned-projectile. Wood dust can cause serious respiratory irritation, so a dust mask is a good idea.

Perform a dry run of each router cut to make sure you can control the machine through the entire cut.

Safety-related maintenance: Tool maintenance is an important aspect of safety, particularly when it comes to collets and bits. Always keep your collets and bits clean, and check them regularly for wear and damage. As for general tool maintenance, caring for the height-adjustment mechanism will ensure smooth, reliable service with fewer surprises. Don't operate a router if it vibrates more than normal or makes an unusual noise; stop and try to diagnose the problem by checking the bit, collet, and motor bearings. See Maintaining Your Router, page 21, and Maintaining Your Bits, page 36 for more maintenance information.

Dry run: After you've completed your setup, loaded the bit, adjusted for depth, and locked everything down, do a quick test run: Slide the router's base along the workpiece a few inches, mimicking the cut. Check your stance and body position to make sure you'll remain balanced during the entire operation without having to overextend to finish the pass. Know where your fingers will be— if both hands aren't on the handles, make sure your fingers can't roam into the cutter. Finally, make sure that the cord won't be a hindrance and that no clamps will interfere with the router. All of this will take only a few seconds, so it's well worth the time spent.

Regardless of the type of cut, always start the router motor with the bit away from the workpiece.

RULES OF SAFE ROUTING

- Wear safety glasses and ear protection.
- Unplug the tool when changing bits and before leaving the work area.
- Confirm that the bit, height settings, and workpiece clamps are tight.
- Make a test run before routing to check the setup.
- Hold the router on the work surface with the bit away from the wood when switching on or off.
- Never force the router or workpiece during an operation.
- Never remove more material than is recommended in the owner's manual.

TIP: EASY-OFF

With routers that don't have a trigger-style switch, it can be difficult to see whether the power switch is off, or to remember which position is ON and which is OFF. But a simple modification can help. Mark the OFF direction with an arrow, a piece of tape or dab of paint, or the word "OFF" on the OFF side of the switch.

Starting up: Before starting the router, make sure the base is firmly set on the workpiece and the bit is an inch or so away from the wood. If you start up with the bit contacting the wood, it can grab and jerk the tool from your hands. Also, routers tend to jump when started (especially those without the soft start feature), so keeping the bit at a safe distance is a critical practice. Always wait for the router to reach full speed before initiating the cut. When routing, turn off the tool immediately if something seems fishy. It could be a dull or loose bit, the wrong bit, a worn collet, or any number of problems.

Router bits only: Just as your eighth-grade shop teacher told you, never chuck anything into the router collet other than a router bit. Drill bits and attachments aren't made for the extreme operating conditions that a router imposes. A foreign tool could easily break and become a wayward missile.

When routing acrylic, leave the protective paper on both sides. Check manufacturer's recommendations for bits and bit speeds.

Materials & Stock Preparation

In addition to wood, routers can cut a variety of materials, including plastic (both laminate and acrylic sheets), fiberglass, non-ferrous metals, solid-surface, and drywall. The most important factor in working with non-wood products is using the right bit at the proper speed. Some manufacturers make specialty bits for specific materials, particularly plastic laminate and solid-surface, and they often recommend straight, carbide bits for many other materials. Burr bits are commonly used for fiberglass and some metals. Because bits are designed for specific applications, it's best to contact the manufacturer for help with using their bits on a given project.

Manufactured sheet goods include MDF-core plywood (top), plycore plywood (middle), and lumber-core plywood (bottom).

Routers are used on all types of solid wood, as well as manufactured wood materials, like plywood, medium-density fiberboard (MDF), particleboard, and hardboard. As all woodworkers know, machining solid wood is fraught with small challenges—thanks to Mother Nature—and routing is no exception. Routing requires stock that is straight, square, and flat. Joinery and router table work are particularly sensitive to stock imperfections.

If your workshop isn't equipped with milling tools (table saw, jointer, planer), you can do some limited milling with a router. Jointing edges and squaring wide boards and panels are basic tasks accomplished with a straight bit and a straightedge guide (see Chapter 5) or with a router table (see Chapter 4). For most other millwork, like surfacing and thickness planing, you'll have to have it done at a shop.

Understanding wood types and knowing how to deal with grain variations come with experience. In general, softwoods rout more easily and faster than hardwoods, but not necessarily more cleanly. Tearout is an ever-present problem with any type of wood, but there are several things you can do to minimize it. You'll also find that your router works harder and can burn more easily when cutting across the grain than when cutting with it. Experience will teach you how to adjust the feed rate for different situations.

Manufactured sheet goods come with few of the inconsistencies and dimension concerns of solid wood. Plywood is prone to tearout, however; when cutting plywood, work in accordance with the grain direction of the outer veneers. All sheet goods can burn easily if not properly fed. MDF machines very nicely. It

Warped, bowed, or crowned stock will spoil your best efforts at making precise cuts.

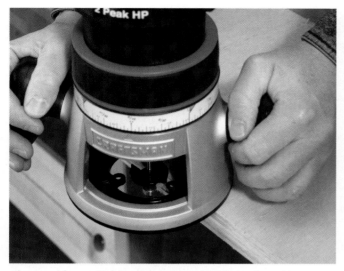

Plywood has reliable dimensions (thickness) and machines well. Standard-grade material may have voids and inconsistencies among the layers that can interfere with edge-forming.

A simple platform clamped to a workbench elevates the routing surface to a more comfortable height.

has no grain or knots to worry about and, unlike plywood, no edge voids, so it's a good material for making templates and jigs.

Setting up the cut: Hand-held routing requires a sturdy bench with lots of room for clamping the workpiece and any fixtures used to control the router. Many people prefer a router work surface that is higher than the average bench, providing a better view of the work without stooping. A simple platform clamped to a bench can raise the work to a comfortable level, and several inches of overhang on any surface helps with clamping. When your bench is ready, you can set up the workpiece and router for a test cut.

Clamping the workpiece. Clamping your work is especially important when routing. Both hands typically are occupied with the tool and can't hold on to the stock, and any slippage of the clamps can ruin the cut, or worse, the workpiece. In most cases, standard clamps will do the job, provided they don't block the router's path. Alternative hold-downs include hot glue, double-sided tape, and non-slip router pads.

When using conventional woodworking clamps it's a good practice to use two or more clamps whenever possible. This keeps the workpiece from rotating—by itself, even a powerful C-clamp is vulnerable to rotation, especially on smooth work surfaces. The basic clamps used for most routing work are shown at right.

Tools for clamping include: squeeze-type clamp (A), hand-screw clamp (B), bar clamp (C), pipe clamp (D), pad-type bar clamp (E), picture frame clamp (F), quick-release bar clamp (G), C-clamp (H), spring clamp (I), and strap clamp (J).

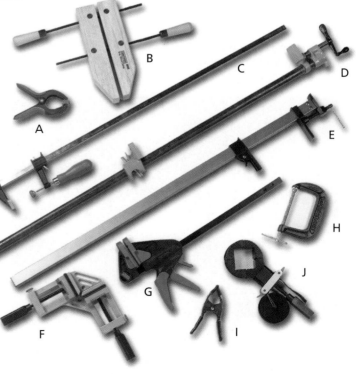

Hot glue can be an excellent clamp for small workpieces. Apply a pea-size dot every 5".

Place the hot-glued workpiece on a larger scrap piece. Clamp the larger piece to the workbench before routing.

Hot glue can provide effective clamping for small stock when a conventional clamp would be in the way. This technique is reliable in situations where the router is helping to hold down the workpiece—do not use it when the strength of conventional clamps is needed or when slippage can be dangerous. To clamp with hot glue, apply a pea-size dab about every 5" along the workpiece, then quickly place the stock onto a supporting surface and hold it for a moment until the glue cools. If the workpiece is too small to support the router base safely, use a stabilizer board of the same thickness secured next to the workpiece. After routing, free the work with an old kitchen knife, then scrape off the residual glue using a metal scraper. A word of warning: hot glue can stick so well that it takes a chunk of the stock with it as you separate the pieces. MDF and plywood are especially prone to this.

A non-slip router pad holds small workpieces in place.

Two types of quickie clamps that work well are double-sided carpet tape and non-slip router pads. Router pads are rubber mats that provide friction to keep the workpiece from sliding. They're effective for jobs in which the router stays on top of the work and there's little sideways pressure, but they are not as safe as clamps.

Loading the Bit & Setting Bit Depth

Always unplug the router before loading or removing a bit. To load a bit, loosen the collet and make sure it's clean inside. Make sure the bit shank is clean, insert the shank into the collet until it bottoms out, then pull it back out about ⅛". At least ¾" of the shank should be inside the collet. Any portion of the shaft that is cut away (at the tops of the flutes) or flared (where the shaft meets the cutter body) should not be inside the collet. Tighten the collet snugly by hand, then tighten it using the collet wrenches (or one wrench if the router has a shaft lock). For two-wrench systems on fixed-base routers, it's easier (and safer for your knuckles) to lay the motor sideways and use the bench to hold one of the wrenches in place while you crank the other by hand. Or, you can use a one-handed scissors method. Tighten the collet firmly, but do not overtighten.

The exact procedure for setting the bit depth is specific to the type and model of router, but the basic steps are similar.

Setting fixed-base bit depth: For all fixed-base routers, the bit depth equals the amount of cutter that is exposed below the surface of the subbase. An easy and accurate way to set the depth is by using a depth gauge tool. With the router unplugged and upside down on your workbench, raise the bit until it touches the gauge's flange, then tighten the base clamping mechanism to lock the motor in place.

Another method is to set the depth by sight. Place the router on the workpiece so the bit clears the piece's edge. Lower the bit to the desired depth, then lock the motor in place. A third method is to use the router's "zero-out" feature (if it has one), following the same procedure used for zeroing-out a plunge router (see below).

Tighten a two-wrench collet by bracing the lower wrench against a workbench and pushing down on the upper wrench. Using an open hand will prevent you from hurting your knuckles.

Two-wrench collets can also be tightened by gripping both wrenches like scissors and squeezing. Hold the motor body steady with the other hand.

Tighten a single-wrench collet by depressing the shaft lock with one hand and tightening the collet with the other.

A router bit depth gauge gives a quick and accurate depth check.

If you don't have a depth gauge, draw a line to mark the bottom of the cut and align the bottom of the cutter blade with the line.

Setting plunge bit depth: To adjust a plunge router, start with the unplugged tool upright on top of the workpiece. Plunge the motor down until the bit just touches the work surface, then engage the plunge lock to keep the motor in place. If the tool has a turret stop, rotate it so the lowest setting is in line with the depth stop rod. Drop the stop rod until it contacts the turret stop, and lock it in place. Next, zero-out the depth setting by moving the depth cursor to "zero" on the scale. Using the cursor as a gauge, raise the stop rod to the desired depth, then lock it in place. Release the plunge lock, and you're ready to rout.

To make the cut incrementally, rotate the turret stop to the highest setting before starting the router. After each pass, retract the bit from the cut and rotate the turret to the next-lowest setting until you reach full depth.

Begin setting a plunge router by zeroing the cursor. With the bit touching the wood, the turret stop at the lowest setting, and the depth stop touching the turret, set the cursor to zero.

To set the desired cutting depth, use the cursor as a gauge to raise the stop rod to the desired depth.

SETTING DEPTH FOR PROFILE CUTS

An easy way to see what you'll be cutting away with a decorative edge-forming bit is to use a scrap cut from the workpiece material. Unplug the router and place the scrap on the router base so its edge touches the bit's pilot bearing. The cutter's profile will show what the cut will look like.

HOW DEEP SHOULD THE CUT BE?

Proper cutting depth—for each pass—is determined by the material; the size, type, and sharpness of the bit; and by the power of the router motor. Cutting too deeply stresses the motor and bit and may burn the wood and prematurely dull the bit. It can also be unsafe because the bit can grab too much wood and cause you to lose control. On the other hand, overly shallow cuts are prudent but may require many passes to reach the finished depth. Knowing the right depth for each cut is something that comes through experience, but here are some general guidelines to follow, based on a mid-size, hand-held router:

• Limit edge-forming cuts to the equivalent of ⅜" square of material. That translates to a ⅜" cutting depth for a ⅜" rabbeting bit, or a ¼" depth for a ½" straight bit.

• Cut wide grooves and dadoes in ⅛"-deep increments.

• Take about ¹⁄₁₆" in the first pass when flush-trimming stock at full thickness.

• Make very light passes—¹⁄₁₆" or so—when using large bits that remove a lot of material, such as raised panel cutters.

Some cuts, such as dovetails, must be made at full depth, but often you can remove the bulk of material first with a straight bit if you feel the cut is too much for the router. Heavy-duty routers can remove more material with less trouble than mid-size tools, although they still are limited by the bit's capability. In any case, it's a good practice to go light on the first pass when routing new material.

Progressively deeper cuts may take more time, but will result in better bit and router performance.

Making Test Cuts

Making test cuts is an essential step with most routing applications. Even after a careful setup, you won't know exactly how the cut will go until you try it out. The test cut also gives you a feel for the setup and how the wood reacts to the bit, which is your best indicator for finding the proper feed rate. Much of routing is a trial-and-error process of making fine adjustments followed by test cuts. To avoid ruining good material, make your test cuts on scrap pieces or on an end of the stock that can be cut off if necessary.

Feeds & Tool Speeds

The direction and rate at which you move the router through a cut are critical factors in the quality of the work. These variables are referred to as the *feed direction* and *feed rate*, respectively, or either may simply be called the *feed*. Another factor that is equally important in certain situations is the tool speed; that is, the rotational speed of the router bit—a factor that can be controlled only on variable-speed routers. There are a few rules of thumb for determining the correct feeds and speeds, but, as with all woodworking techniques, experience is the best teacher.

Note: The feed directions shown here are for hand-held routing. When table routing, all directions are reversed, because the bit is spinning upside down. See Chapter 4 for more information on feeding with table routers.

Feed direction: There are two ways you can feed the router: the conventional feed and a feed that is known as the *climb cut*. The conventional feed moves the router opposite to the work forces of the rotating bit. In hand-held routing, the bit spins clockwise when viewed from above, so the router is fed from left to right. This is the safer method of the two because the force of the router is countered by the force of the operator, resulting in a more balanced, controlled motion. For most routing, the conventional feed direction is the proper method.

The climb cut goes with the bit's rotational force as the router is moved from right to left. With the bit pulling it along, the router has a tendency to climb away from you (hence the name), making it much more difficult to control the tool. Despite this disadvantage, the climb cut is commonly used for select operations because it produces less tearout than conventional feeding and offers a smoother finish with some difficult woods. However, it is considered a dangerous practice and should always be done with care and a great deal of awareness. Always make a very light pass when climb cutting, to minimize the potential for the bit to grab the wood and pull the router.

Feed rate: The ideal feed rate for any cut is based on five main factors: 1) the material (its hardness, density, grain properties, etc.), 2) the router bit (characteristics such as size, number of flutes, sharpness, and cutter complexity), 3) the depth of the cut (see How Deep Should the Cut Be, page 49), 4) the power of the router motor, and 5) the tool speed. Generally, hard wood, large bits, deep cuts, and less power require slower feed rates.

CONVENTIONAL FEED DIRECTIONS

The conventional feed moves the router opposite to the work forces of the rotating bit. In hand-held routing, the bit spins clockwise when viewed from above, so the router is fed from left to right. This is the safer method of the two because the force of the router is countered by the force of the operator, resulting in a more balanced, controlled motion. For most routing, the conventional feed direction is the proper method.

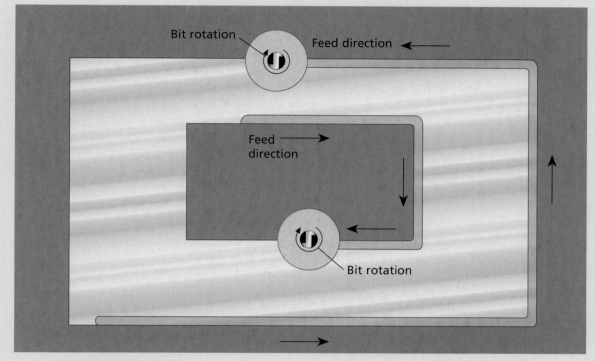

Bit rotation

Feed direction

Feed direction

Bit rotation

Inside and outside edge cuts

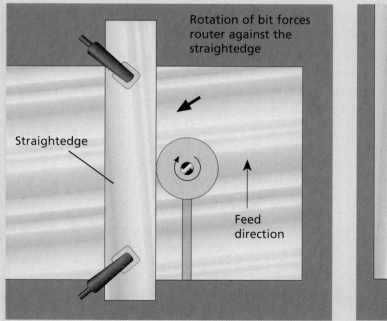

Rotation of bit forces router against the straightedge

Straightedge

Feed direction

Cuts using a straightedge

Bit rotation pulls router away from edge and holds guide against stock

Feed direction

Cuts using an edge guide

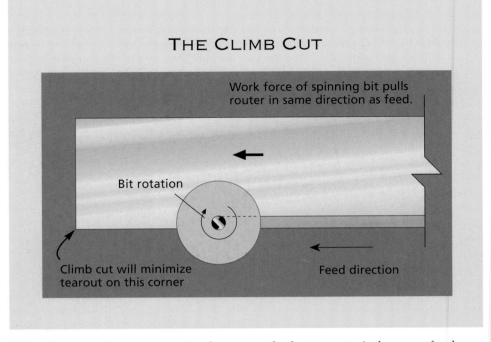

THE CLIMB CUT

Work force of spinning bit pulls router in same direction as feed.

Bit rotation

Climb cut will minimize tearout on this corner

Feed direction

When it comes down to routing, however, the best way to judge your feed rate is by the quality of the cut. Feeding the router too fast stresses the motor and bit and typically produces a rough cut, torn fibers, or excessive tearout. And the motor will sound overloaded if the feed rate is too fast. Feeding too slowly creates excessive friction, resulting in burnishing or burn marks in the wood. Your test cuts will tell you whether your feed rate is good. Once you start making the real cut, it's important to keep the feed rate constant. If you stop moving the router or slow down too much, even for an instant, the wood will burn.

Tool speed: Standard routers run at an average speed of about 24,000 rpm. This rate is acceptable for most router bits up to about 1" in diameter. Bits 1" and larger typically require slower speeds, because the greater diameter translates to more travel along the wood at a faster rate. Thus a slower spin is needed to ensure safety and prevent burning. To run large bits, you must use a router with variable speed, which can be set at anywhere from 8,000 to 24,000 rpm, on average. Bit manufacturers often recommend a tool speed for their larger bits. The chart below shows general guidelines for safe routing speeds. Note that bits over 1¾" in diameter should by used only on a router table.

SAFE TOOL SPEEDS

BIT DIAMETER	MAXIMUM TOOL SPEED
Up to 1"	24,000 rpm
1¼" to *2"	18,000 rpm
*2¼" to 2½"	16,000 rpm
*2¾" to 3½"	12,000 rpm
*recommended for router table use only.	

Practicing on scrap wood will help you determine the correct feed rate. The hard oak (left) and soft pine (right) show the results of cutting too slow (top), too fast (middle), and just right (bottom).

Troubleshooting Poor Cuts

Problems with router cuts can be due to several factors, including operator error, poorly milled material, improper setups, and using the wrong bit or router for the job. Some problems, namely burning and tearout, are common pitfalls that are linked to the router's design, and avoiding them requires constant vigilance. Listed here are some of the most common cutting flaws and suggestions for correcting them.

Burning

• Make sure bits are sharp (see Marks of a dull bit, page 37).

• Don't hesitate during the cut. Pay special attention to points where you naturally tend to slow down, especially at the beginning or end of a cut and when routing around corners. Also try starting with a sweeping motion (see Tip: A Sweeping Start, page 55).

• Make light passes. Cutting too deeply in a single pass forces a slower feed rate, which commonly leads to burning.

• Remove burn marks by making an additional light pass with the router, if you can afford to remove the extra material. The alternative is

Cutting across the grain can often result in edge tearout.

Clamping a sacrificial board on the exit side of a cross-grain cut will prevent tearout.

sanding, which is difficult at best and often impossible on end grain.

Tearout

• When cutting across the grain, clamp a sacrificial piece of wood as a backer to the exit side of the cut.

• When routing the perimeter of a board, or adjacent perpendicular sides, make the cross-grain cuts first. This allows you to clean up the tearout when you make the long-grain cuts.

• Prevent top-side tearout (usually a fuzz) from making a rough ride for the router by using a template or straight-edge and a template guide (see Chapter 7). This lifts the router subbase off the surface of the workpiece for a smoother ride and cleaner cut.

• Use a sharper bit and make lighter passes.

Problems with bearing-guided bits

• When a cut is flawed due to a rough workpiece edge, either clean up the edge and re-rout, or switch to a setup with a straightedge guide and a pattern bit or template guide. A base-mounted edge guide can help bridge minor dips in the workpiece edge.

Dips and bumps in the workpiece (like this knot) will transfer to the router cut. Either smooth the workpiece or use a straightedge guide instead of a bearing bit.

• If the uncut edge of a workpiece is burnished or scored, check the travel of the bearing, and replace it if necessary. Don't use edging bits with solid pilots.

• When rounding over the top and bottom of plywood, make sure the bearing is indexing from the same surface. Inconsistencies in the plies can produce poor results.

• Avoid deflection or runout from long, skinny, flush-trimming bits by switching to a pattern bit or template guide setup.

TIP: A SWEEPING START

When starting an edge cut, it's easy to leave a burn mark if you push the router straight in until the base contacts the edge guide or bearing, then move it sideways to make the cut. There's just enough hesitation to burn the wood. Instead, start with a curved, sweeping motion so that the bit reaches its full cutting position a few inches from the end of the workpiece. Run to the end of the cut using the same feed direction. Complete the cut by returning to the beginning and making a second pass, again sweeping into the workpiece but with an opposite feed direction, to finish off the first few inches. Typically this final pass is a climb cut, so be careful. Make sure the router base is supported by the board at the beginning of the motion.

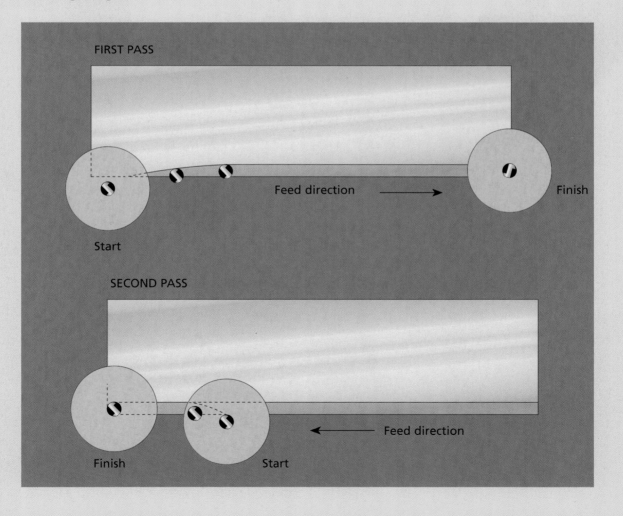

Chapter 4
TABLE ROUTING

Router tables add considerably to the versatility of routing. With the tool secured below the table and the bit exposed above, you can use both hands to run the workpiece past the bit, often without hold-downs or special clamping. The fence provides the means for controlling the cut, just like a table saw fence does. Together with the flat, stable surface of the tabletop, the fence allows for safe, accurate cuts with quick setup (many cuts require only two settings—bit depth and fence adjustment). Using a bearing-guided bit, you can rout without a fence and take advantage of the tabletop's broad surface for support. A basic shop-made version can be inexpensive and easy to build, and may be all you'll ever need. Or you can buy one of the many commercial tables available.

Advantages of Table Routing

While router tables aren't ideal for every task, the great majority of work done by hand-held routers can also be accomplished on the table, and often more safely and efficiently than with a portable tool. Which setup is better for a specific job? The deciding factor in many cases is the size of the workpiece: if it's too small to support the base of a hand-held router, consider working on the table; if it's too big to maneuver easily on the table, use a hand-held router.

Tables clearly are the better choice (and in some cases, the only choice), when routing with large bits. As a general rule, bits over 1¾" in diameter are much safer to use in table-mounted routers. Big bits can be hard to control with hand-held routers, especially on edge-forming operations. When using large bits on the router table, cover as much of the bit as possible with the fence, and cut incrementally with light passes. Also make sure to adjust the tool's speed based on the bit's diameter (see Safe Tool Speeds, page 52) or as recommended by the bit manufacturer. Many large bits are designed for use in a router table only.

It is recommended that large, complex cutters like this lock-miter bit be used in router tables only. With a hand-held tool, the slightest tipping would ruin the cut and possibly kick back the work.

Having a fence to work from offers several advantages. First, it keeps the work-piece in line and allows you to focus on the feed and other critical aspects—in contrast to hand-held operations, where you have to remain constantly aware of keeping the router upright. A tall fence provides support for running work-pieces on-edge or vertically, simplifying cuts that would require complicated setups for hand-held work. The fence controls the depth of cut when using non-piloted bits but can also produce superior results with bearing-guided cut-ters. By setting the fence just in front of the bearing, you eliminate the transfer of defects from the workpiece edge to the cut.

Building Your Own Router Table

The essential design criteria for any router table are simple: The table must be smooth and flat, and the fence must be straight and square to the table. As long as those requirements are met, you can use almost any materials and include any features you like. Shown here are the basic components of a router table and some suggestions for building your own table. Woodworking catalogs and magazines often feature router table plans and tips for customizing a table for your particular needs. There's also a list of accessories that you can add to a basic table as your work warrants.

Base: First you'll need to plan the type of base your table will have. One option is to go without a base. That is, simply to use a tabletop surface clamped to a workbench, saw table, or other work surface. The tabletop may be as large as you need, but is easily stored on edge anywhere in your shop.

A second option is to build a short, free-standing base. This is called a benchtop table and is the most portable type. At about 15" high, a benchtop table can be stored out of the way when not in use and can be carried on-site and set up any-

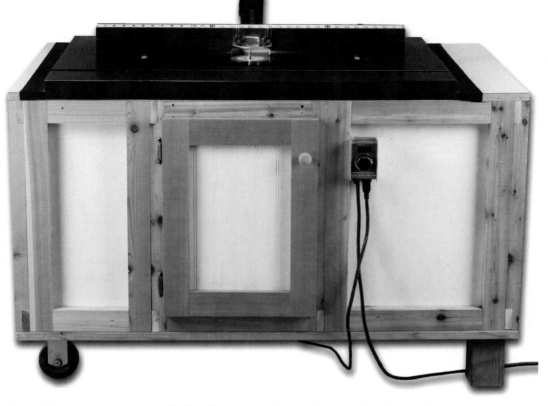

A shop-made router table and base built using parts available from woodworking catalogs.

where. Make certain you include a lip or overhang than can be clamped to the benchtop.

A floor table is the closest thing to a stationary tool, with a full-height tabletop and often a partially enclosed cabinet or drawers below. A key advantage of a floor table is that it's a dedicated work station that's ready to go when you are (especially if you have an extra base mounted to the tabletop; see Dedicating a Base, page 64). Adding wheels makes it easier to move the table around the shop if need be.

Tabletop: The most popular tabletop materials are sheet goods, including MDF, plywood, particleboard, hardboard, and acrylic. For a smooth, durable finish, you can laminate the top with plastic laminate, or buy thick, melamine-coated particleboard. Plywood and bare particleboard typically need some kind of lamination or can be sandwiched between layers of ¼"-thick hardboard for smoothness. MDF is smooth enough to stand alone but should be finished with an appropriate oil or other wood finish for durability and to prevent moisture damage. Any finish or laminate applied to the top side must also go on the bottom side, to prevent warping.

Tabletops can be made of two layers of ½" plywood and a ¼" hardboard layer on top and bottom (top); ⅝" MDF supported with 2× lumber (middle); or 1"- to 1¼"-thick melamine-coated particleboard with edge banding (bottom).

The thickness of the top depends on the table's design. A basic clamp-on tabletop must be stiff enough to be cantilevered over the edge of a bench without flexing, so a 1"-thick wood top is a good starting point. Benchtop and floor tables can have a supporting structure of wood crosspieces underneath and be made with ⅝" or thicker MDF or with a core of ¾" plywood. A ⅜"-thick acrylic top, provided it's well supported, makes a very smooth, flat table surface.

Keep in mind that thicker tops have the drawback of limiting the bit depth. There are a few remedies for this problem: you can recess the base into the bottom side of the top, switch to a thinner top with a support frame instead of a thick laminated top, or use a mounting plate (see Mounting plates, page 63).

A basic board fence can be clamped to the router table. To create the bit cutout, clamp one end to the tabletop and rotate the other end over the spinning bit.

Tabletop size is a matter of personal choice, but the sizes of commercial tables can give you some ideas: benchtop models average 16" to 18" wide and 20" to 24" long; floor models have bigger tops, about 24" wide and 32" to 44" long. A clamp-on tabletop should have some extra material behind the bit for clamping to the supporting surface. Consider the amount of room available in

This L-shaped fence is readily made from ¾" plywood. Make sure the fence makes a right angle with the tabletop. A pivot bolt with knob allows for quick adjustments.

Surrounding the Bit

Using the tabletop and fence to enclose the bit as much as possible improves safety and performance. It prevents the workpiece from getting hung up or pulled into the space around the bit, it improves stability, and it reduces tearout, especially with large specialty bits. If you own large bits, it's a good idea to make more than one tabletop, each with a bit hole to accommodate a different range of bit sizes. Some commercial mounting plates have reducer rings for closing in on different sizes of bits as shown here.

For an average range of general-work bits, you can notch a shop-made fence so it just fits around the largest bit. With some specialty bits, it's better to make a zero-clearance fence: using a new fence board or a sacrificial board secured in front of your regular fence, clamp the fence at one end and carefully pivot the fence into the spinning bit to cut an exact profile of the bit.

your shop and the sorts of items you will be routing. If you know you'll be routing small items, a small tabletop may be sufficient.

Securing the router to the top: There are a couple of options for mounting the router. If you're using a fixed-base router, the simplest method is to remove the plastic subbase and mount the base casting directly to the tabletop with machine bolts run through the top and into the base. When using a plunge router, most people like to mount the router base to a mounting plate that fits into a recessed window in the tabletop. This allows you to pull the router from the table for bit changes and depth adjustments. You can buy a commercial mounting plate or make your own from ⅜" acrylic.

Locate the router in a position that best suits your work. The hole where the bit comes through should be centered along the length of the table, but its position relative to the width of the table is up to you. Also consider access to the router motor when determining the hole position.

Fence: A fence can be as simple as a board clamped to the table or as complex as a split-fence with two sides that can be adjusted independently, like the infeed and outfeed tables of a jointer. A basic L-shape is a good compromise, made with two pieces of plywood or hardwood, glued perpendicular to each other and supported behind with square-angle brackets. This type of fence offers easy clamping along the flat base piece and a secure vertical piece for running workpieces in a variety of configurations. A pivot bolt at one end of the fence simplifies adjustments.

As mentioned, a good fence must be straight and square to the table for reliable cuts. Periodically check your fence with a straightedge, and adjust or re-joint it as needed to keep it in line. Simple fences are considered disposable by many router users; they're simply replaced when they're worn out or no longer work well.

Router Table Accessories

Accessories can make your router table safer, more versatile, and tailored to the type of work you do. Many accessories are available commercially through router and woodworking tool manufacturers and mail-order woodworking catalogs. You can also build your own copies of commercial designs or create custom features.

Bit guards: These basic safety devices protect your fingers and other body parts from the spinning bit. They are especially necessary when routing using a bearing-guided bit without a fence. Custom guards are easy to make with ¼"-thick clear acrylic. Making a few different styles will ensure that you have a guard for most router table operations. Four inches of coverage is adequate protection for most bits.

Commercial bit guards are often packaged with fences, but are also sold separately to be attached to a shop-made fence. Some bit guards, like those for fenceless routing, are combined with a dust port.

Base-mounted switches: Base-mounted switches are handy features that increase safety by allowing you to turn your table router on and off without having to reach under the table. All it takes is some basic wiring. Mount two receptacle boxes (one for a receptacle, one for a switch) to the base, then run NM cable between the boxes. Run a grounded appliance cable from the receptacle box so you can plug it into the nearest receptacle outlet. Install a duplex receptacle in one box and a single-pole switch in the other, and make the wiring connections. Be sure to mount both boxes in a convenient location—even with the switch system, you should unplug the router for bit changes. Protect the switch from accidental bumps by mounting it inside the base or within a recess on the outside.

A flat acrylic bit guard attached to a board is a quick and easy bit guard and fence combination.

Other switch options are available. An adjustable-speed switch allows you to convert a single-speed router motor into a variable-speed router. This is especially handy for table routing where you are more likely to use the larger bits which require slower speeds. Also available are lockout switches which allow you to lock or remove the switch to prevent unauthorized use, and oversized stop switches, which are easy to hit in a hurry.

Mounting plates: An alternative to mounting the router base directly to the table is to use a mounting plate. You can create your own mounting plate with ⅜" acrylic. Cut the smallest size square hole your router base will fit in (handles usually can be removed for clearance if necessary) in your tabletop. Then rout a ½"-wide by ⅜"-deep rabbet around the hole to create a lip for the plate. Cut the plate to size and drill the bit opening (1¼" is a good starting size) and the mounting screw holes. The top must be rabbeted perfectly so the plate lies flush with no side-to-side movement. Any variation between the plate and the table surface can affect your cuts (dust and chips collecting in the rabbet are another nuisance).

Mounting plates are available commercially with several nice features, including starting pins (see Routing without a fence, page 73), predrilled holes for the router base, leveling screws (to help keep the plate flush with the tabletop), and reducer rings to match a variety of bit sizes. Some plates even come with a template guide for template work on the table. Better commercial plates are made from machined metal or phenolic resin and come as a blank with only the bit hole, or pre-drilled to fit specific router models.

Make an adjustable L-shaped guard by gluing acrylic parts together and screwing them onto the fence. Slots allow for height adjustment.

A switch mounted on the router table base makes turning a table router on and off much easier and safer.

A router lift allows you to insert a hand crank into the mounting plate to adjust the bit height from above the table.

A miter gauge slot on a router table can be used to hold clamps and featherboards. Or, you can use your table saw miter (set at 90°) to support work as you push it past the bit.

A "MUST" FOR PLUNGE ROUTERS

A fine-depth adjuster (or micro-adjust) takes the hassle out of setting bit depth on table-mounted plunge routers. This inexpensive accessory attaches to the router and has a long shaft that's easy to reach. Check with the manufacturer for an adjuster made for your router. Adjusters are also available for some fixed-base routers.

Mounting plates do require a large hole in the tabletop, which can weaken it. If you're using a plunge router in your table, however, a plate adds a lot of convenience because you can pull the plate and router up through the top of the table to change bits.

Miter gauge slots: Modeled after the same slot on a table saw, miter gauge slots are features some people want on a router table. Slots allow you to use a commercial miter gauge. This is especially handy for moving the ends of mitered stock past the bit. The slot also provides an anchoring point for featherboards and other fixtures. Critics of the miter slot say they mar and can weaken the tabletop, and that a miter gauge isn't the best way to guide their work. As alternatives to a slot and miter gauge, you can secure featherboards with clamps or threaded inserts set into the table and use a simple sled to guide workpieces (see Rules of Safe Table Routing, page 72).

Router lifts: These mechanisms carry the router below the table and allow you to adjust the bit height from above, using a hand crank or other tool. Most types are anchored to a mounting plate that fits into a rabbeted window just like a standard mounting plate. Some lifts accept only fixed-base routers and others

DEDICATING A BASE

If you're using a mid-size fixed base router in your table, buy an extra base and leave it permanently mounted to the table. Some manufacturers offer a simplified, handleless base for this purpose.

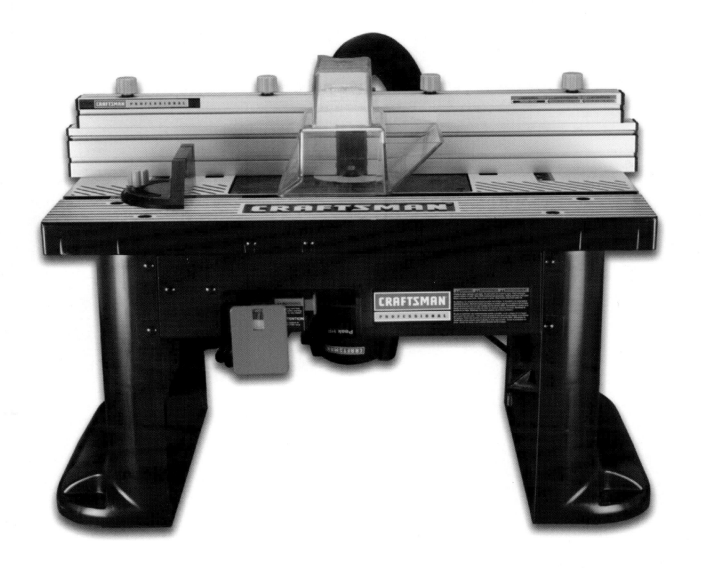

only plunge. A few models have the ability to raise the motor high enough to change bits from above the table. Router lifts can easily cost more than the router itself. They do add convenience but don't really improve the performance of a table router.

Compact and portable, a benchtop table can be carried and set up anywhere. An overhanging base piece is handy for clamping to a benchtop.

Commercial Router Tables

Commercial tables are available as clamp-on tabletop, benchtop, and floor models. In terms of quality, the overall field runs wide, as does the price range. When shopping, look closely at the main components—the tabletop, the fence, and the base—and compare the usability features, such as fence adjustments and overall versatility. There are a lot of great tables to choose from, as well as a few design features to avoid. Safety features, like bit guards, starting pins, and reducer rings, should be available as accessories if they aren't standard equipment.

Tabletops: Most commercial tops are made with thick MDF covered with plastic laminate or melamine. Aluminum is a fairly common material, and a few tables are made with steel. At the high end are a few tables made with phenolic resin,

Good MDF tops have high-pressure laminate on both sides and protective edging. Before using any new table, check the top for flatness. Return it if it fails the test.

A one-piece fence with all the good features: T-slot (with sacrificial wood fence attached), tool-free adjustments, and vacuum port.

a nearly indestructible plastic that's guaranteed to stay flat. Phenolic is the best all-around material but comes with a high price tag. Metal tables are strong and stay flat, but some require maintenance to prevent rusting; aluminum can leave that familiar gray residue on wood. The better MDF tops are fairly trouble-free, provided they are laminated on both sides and are protected along the edges with a rubber strip or other edging.

Router mounts: Except for light-duty benchtop tables, most commercially available tables come with mounting plate systems. Make sure the plate fits perfectly in the window and has leveling screws for keeping the top flush. Routers may be centered within the top or offset towards the front or back edge. On tables with an offset configuration, a fence that can be used on either side of the router adds versatility.

Commercial benchtop router tables are often direct mount and often brand specific. Before buying a benchtop table that is not produced by the

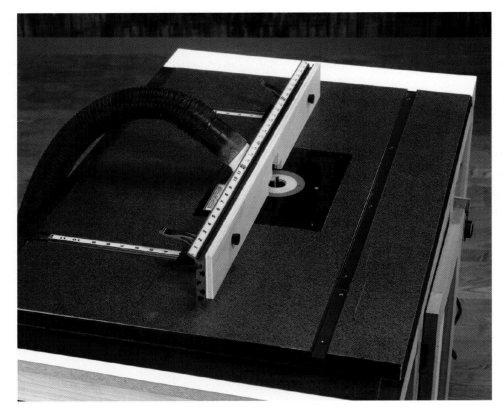

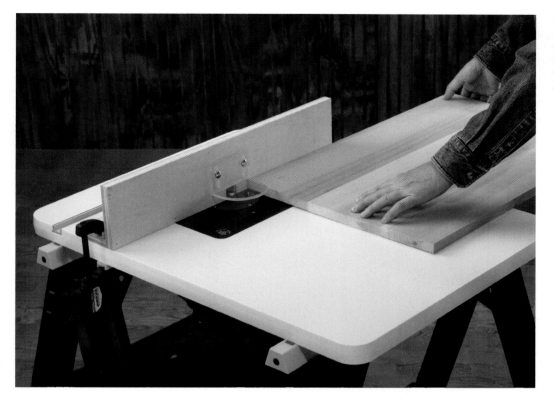

With an offset router mount, moving the fence to the narrow side of the table gives you the broad support of the wider side.

same company as your router, check the mounting screw compatibility. Commercial tabletops are available with mounting plates to accommodate the major router models. If you can't locate one to fit your router, blank plates are also available. You simply drill mounting holes to fit your router base.

If the upper part of a cabinet base is enclosed with doors, you can run a vacuum hose into the back to collect accumulated dust and chips.

Fences: Good tables have metal fences and several useful features. Fence designs are either one-piece (meaning one long stick) or two-piece (with independent fence surfaces set to either side of the bit). One-piece fences are simpler and easier to adjust in many cases. Two-piece designs let you offset the infeed and outfeed sides for edge-jointing and allow you to close in the fence around the bit. On the downside, it takes some effort to align the two sides perfectly, which is what you need for most routing operations. A useful feature on either type of fence is a T-slot or other means for attaching a sacrificial wood fence or various hold-downs and fixtures.

Tool-free knobs and clamping devices are preferable to adjustment mechanisms that require

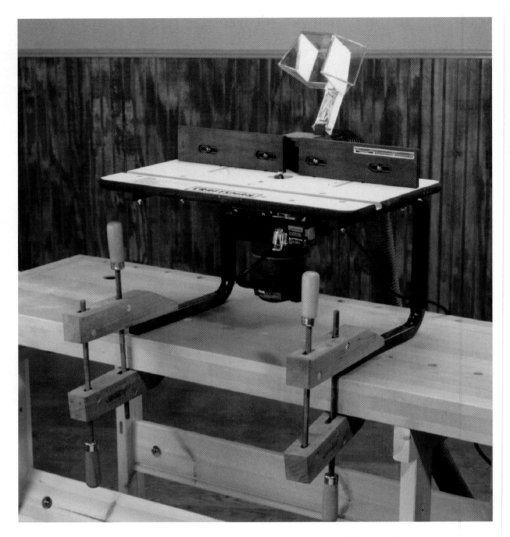

A commercial benchtop table with frame-style open base, flip-up blade guard, two-piece fence, vacuum port, and base-mounted switch. Always clamp the base to the supporting workbench for safest use.

tools. The ability to place the fence anywhere on the table is a plus. And a vacuum port for dust collection is a valuable feature even if you don't yet have a vacuum system.

Base: Base style and features are largely a matter of choice. There are wood cabinet-style bases, metal and wood frame-style bases, and folding-stand bases. Cabinets provide storage space and can help contain dust and reduce tool noise. They also create the sturdiest bases, but are difficult to move around unless they have wheels. Open, frame-style bases are lighter than cabinets, an advantage for benchtop models. Folding bases can be unstable and move during routing— a potentially serious drawback.

Getting Started with Table Routing

Much of the safety and setup information provided in Chapter 3 also applies to router table work. This includes the discussions on material preparation, loading the bit and setting bit depth, tool speed, and general safety precautions. It's important that you review those sections along with the safety and operation procedures given here, which are specific to the router table.

Router table safety: The main safety concerns with table routing involve exposure to the bit, feeding techniques, and trapping the workpiece (which can

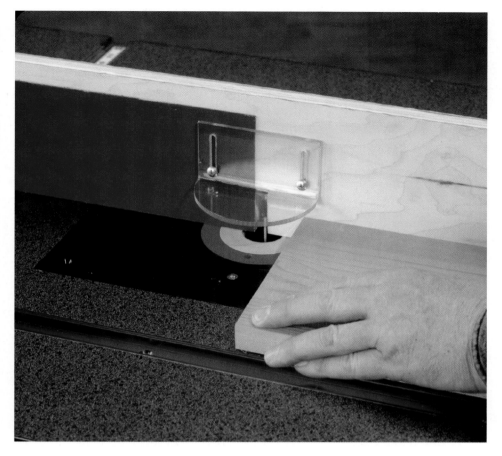

This safe setup includes a bit guard and minimal clearances around the bit. For a full-thickness cut, the bit depth needs to extend only ⅟₁₆" above the top face of the workpiece.

cause kickback and other unpleasant outcomes). Understanding feed directions and keeping your hands away from the cutter are your best defenses against trouble. As with hand-held routing, safe work on the table starts with the setup. If a cut seems tricky or potentially risky, stop and rethink the setup. There's probably a better way to do it, or it might be safer to make the cut with a hand-held router.

Bit safety: You can cover bit safety and reduce exposure risk by following a few rules of thumb. First, set the bit depth to expose only what is necessary to make the cut. Use the fence and proper hole size in the table to close in around the bit as much as possible, and make a zero-clearance fence when appropriate (see Surrounding the Bit, page 61). In all cases where a bit guard can be used, do so (see Bit guards, page 62).

Second, prepare for the unexpected. If you're pushing a workpiece toward the cutter and something slips or the work is suddenly zipped from your grasp, where will your hands go? Stay well balanced during a cut and make sure the force you're applying to the workpiece won't bring your hands near the cutter if something goes wrong. During the cut, the bit is often concealed by the work and can emerge unexpectedly from the end of the workpiece. For this reason, use pushsticks and never your hands to push from the back edge of stock when your fingers could be anywhere near the cutter.

Feed direction: If you're not familiar with the principles of feed direction and feed rate, see Feeds & Tool Speeds, starting on page 50. The conventional feed

direction for router table work is opposite that of hand-held routing for the simple reason that the router is upside down, thus reversing the bit's rotation relative to the user. In hand-held work, the bit spins clockwise and the proper feed is to move the router from left to right over the workpiece. In table routing, the bit spins counterclockwise and the conventional feed is moving the workpiece from right to left along the fence.

With the conventional feed, the working forces of the bit pull the workpiece against the fence and push it back toward you (the user), giving you more control. Feeding left to right is a climb cut, and the bit's action forces the work away from the fence and you. If the bit grabs during a climb cut, it can pull the work from your hands and send your fingers toward the bit. Keeping this in mind, you can make safe climb cuts if you take all measures necessary to control the work and make very light passes.

Trapping the workpiece: Trapping the work between the bit and fence is a dangerous situation that must always be avoided. This creates an especially hazardous climb cut in which the board, pinched between the immovable fence and spinning bit, can be shot across the shop at a ballistic rate. In most situations you'll avoid trapping the workpiece by keeping the work between yourself and the bit.

The standard feed direction using a router table pushes the workpiece against the fence. A climb cut on the router table can grab the workpiece and pull your fingers toward the bit.

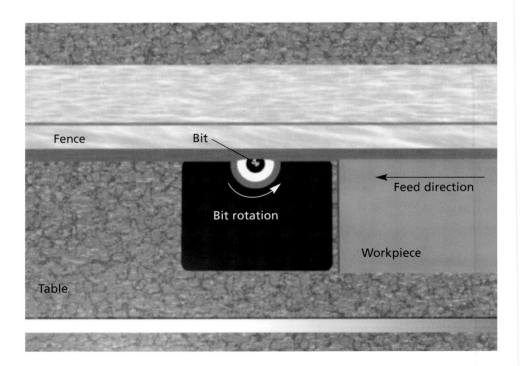

Fence   Bit

Bit rotation

Feed direction

Workpiece

Table

The correct way to cut an edge using a table router and fence. The bit is on the fence-side edge of the board and fingers are protected by the bit guard.

Trapping the wood between the bit and the fence creates a dangerous situation where the wood will be pinched and likely kicked back.

Trapping can happen three different ways. One is setting the fence away from the bit and feeding the board between the fence and the bit (see above, right). The second way trapping happens is when using a router table to widen grooves on a workpiece. This can fool you because while you think you're making a conventional left-to-right feed, you're actually climb cutting and trapping

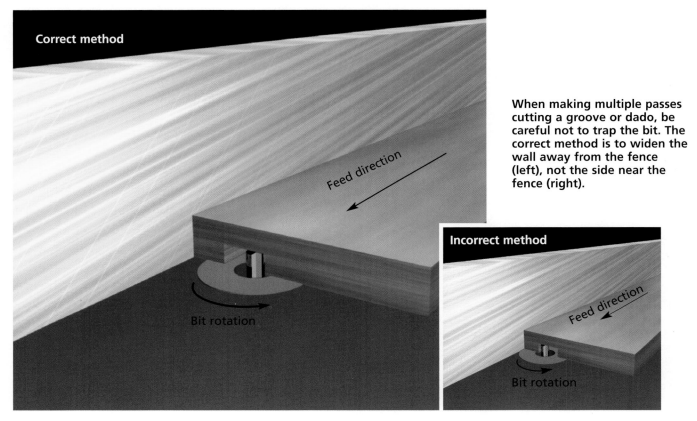

Correct method

Feed direction

Bit rotation

Incorrect method

Feed direction

Bit rotation

When making multiple passes cutting a groove or dado, be careful not to trap the bit. The correct method is to widen the wall away from the fence (left), not the side near the fence (right).

the work against the fence. Avoid this dangerous setup by widening the wall of the groove that is farther from the fence. The third instance of trapping occurs when the bit is raised and the workpiece is fed between the bit and the table-top (see photo page 82).

Basic Router Table Operations

Many of the common techniques used in router table work are described here. Specific table operations, like edge-forming, joinery techniques, and template routing, are covered in their respective chapters.

Hold-downs, push sticks & sleds: Push sticks, sleds, and hold-downs such as featherboards help you push the work safely past the bit and are especially useful for small and narrow stock that might endanger your fingers. A push stick can have almost any design and be made with scrap wood. For narrow work, a solid stick with a notched end will suffice. For routing larger stock, attach a handle to a scrap block (make sure the block has square corners) to make a push sled that doubles as a backer board to prevent tearout. Trim the block or move the handle to a new block when the old one has seen too many cuts. A simple L-shaped sled helps support stock set on-edge. Glue two scrap pieces of plywood or lumber together so they're square, and discard the sled when it gets chewed up. Use featherboards—either shop-made or commercial—anytime a second pair of "hands" can help you keep the work in line.

Featherboards and push sticks improve router safety. Featherboards can be clamped onto the fence or you can use T-bolts and knobs in the miter slot. Push sticks can be purchased or made from scrap lumber.

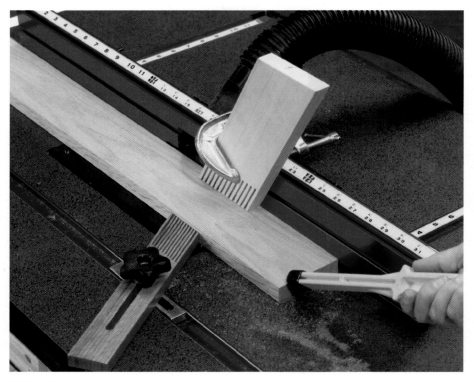

A push sled with a notch safely holds small stock for table routing. A handle grip keeps fingers away from the blade.

An L-shaped sled supports stock on-edge for cuts like this tenon shoulder cut. Because you cannot use a bit guard on these cuts, use clamps to keep your fingers at a safe distance from the bit.

Routing without a fence: Always use a starting pin (or fulcrum) for bearing-guided work without a fence. When initiating a cut into a bearing-guided bit, the cutter can grab the workpiece, resulting in a gouge and possibly yanking the work from your hands. The starting pin helps prevent this by acting as a stabilizing point until the work makes contact with the bit's bearing. Commercial mounting plates often come with a metal or plastic starting pin that threads into the plate. You can add a pin to a shop-made table by installing a threaded insert into the top or by clamping on a pointed board to act as a fulcrum. Locate the starting pin 2" to 4" from the bit. Remember, if a task calls for a starting pin, you should also use a bit guard.

To make the cut, anchor the work against the pin, then carefully pivot it into the bit until it contacts the guide bearing. Complete the cut while keeping the work in contact with the bearing. If convenient, you can use the starting pin for

A starting pin is often standard on commercial mounting plates. A bit guard is a must when doing this type of routing.

If you don't have a starting pin, a pointed board clamped to the tabletop can act as a fulcrum.

To set up for edge-jointing, glue or clamp a plastic laminate shim to the outfeed side of the fence. Use a straight-edge to align the bit's cutting edge with the laminate. This will remove ¹⁄₁₆" of material with each pass.

extra stability, but don't let it distract you from the cut. Be very mindful of feed direction here. Always move the work against the rotation of the bit.

Edge-jointing: Smoothing and squaring up an edge is an easy operation on the router table. To remove about ¹⁄₁₆" of material from an edge of stock, set up a straight bit for a full-thickness cut. Clamp or adhere a plastic laminate shim on the outfeed side of the fence, then set the fence so the bit will cut flush with the laminate face. Run the stock through as many times as needed for a clean, square edge.

To set up a stopped cut on the router table, begin by marking the front and back edges of the bit on the fence and table-top.

Making stopped cuts: A stopped cut is any interior cut that begins or ends at a point inside from the workpiece edge. A blind cut is a stopped cut where both ends stop short of the edge. You can make many types of stopped cuts with accuracy on a router table. However, because blind cuts have no access from the workpiece edge, you must plunge the work down onto the spinning bit to initiate the cut—a potentially risky operation that must be done carefully and always with a stop block as an anchor. As a rule, blind cuts are safer and cleaner with a hand-held plunge router.

To set up a stopped cut on the router table, load the bit (use a plunge-cutting type) and use a straightedge or square block to mark the front and back edges of the bit (plane over from the tips of the cutters). Mark onto the fence or table or onto a piece of tape. On the workpiece, mark the beginning and end of the cut. Line up the leading mark on the workpiece with the left (front) bit mark and clamp a

Line up the workpiece stopping line with the back of the bit. Clamp a stop block in front of the workpiece. Move the workpiece to align the starting line with the front edge of the bit. Clamp a starting block behind the workpiece.

To make the cut, raise the bit to the desired height (it is best to make multiple shallow passes). Place the heel of the workpiece against the starting block and lower the workpiece onto the spinning bit. Slide the workpiece to the stop block. Turn off the machine before lifting the work.

A stopped cut simply requires a stop block rather than both a start and stop block. Feed the workpiece along the fence in normal fashion.

starting block to the fence or table at the trailing end of the workpiece. For blind cuts, line up the other two marks and clamp a stop block at the other end.

For safety, make the cut incrementally with a series of light passes. Anchor the end of the workpiece against the starting block. Keeping the work firm against the fence, slowly pivot it down onto the bit. Once you make contact, move the work back and forth slightly until the bit reaches full depth, then move the work from right to left until it contacts the stop block. Turn the machine off before lifting the work from the bit at the end of the cut. It's critical to keep constant pressure against the fence during all stages of the cut and especially when lifting the work at the end.

TABLE SHIMS

A stack of ⅛" or ¼" MDF or hardboard spacers allows you to make incremental cuts with one depth setting. Set the bit to the desired full depth. Clamp a few spacers to the table (or fence), removing one after each pass until you reach final depth.

Chapter 5
EDGE-FORMING & GUIDE ROUTING

The two categories of work that best define routing are edge-forming and guide routing. Edge-forming is done primarily with bearing-guided bits. It's the simplest type of routing and certainly one of the most satisfying. All that's required for the setup is chucking the bit and setting the depth, and within a few seconds you can turn an ordinary board into a finished work with a classically profiled detail. From there you can move on to decorating the surface of stock with flutes and various ornamental grooves or to making custom molding and trim. Guide routing requires very basic skills and setups but can accomplish a huge range of woodworking tasks—from making dadoes and grooves to trimming and squaring stock to cutting perfect circles.

Decorative Edge-forming

When people ask, "What does a router do?" typically the first answer given is something like, "Shape the edges of wood, for tables or countertops." That, in a nutshell, is decorative edge-forming, and it's what the router does better than any other tool. If you look through a router bit catalog, invariably the largest category of bits is devoted to edge-forming. Most of these bits are bearing-guided. With piloted bits, the bearing determines the side-to-side depth, so all you have to set is the up and down. Edge-forming techniques are simple, but because this is finish work you often get only one chance with a cut. A few practice cuts will help you get the feel of a new bit or stock material before you start the real work.

Edge-forming with hand-held routers: The key to smooth edge-forming lies in keeping even pressure on the bearing against the stock while maintaining the proper feed rate. If you hesitate at corners or the ends of the cut, you'll burn the wood. You also need to keep the router from tipping. In hand-held work, less than half of the sub-base is supported by the workpiece, so it's easy to let the tool tilt sideways and spoil the cut. An offset sub-base provides greater stability than a standard base for edge cuts.

When edge-forming the entire perimeter of a board, start with the cross-grain cuts first. The tearout will be removed when making the long-grain cuts.

If only the cross-grain ends are being routed, use a scrap board clamped firmly against the exit side of the cut to prevent tearout.

Tearout is another vital consideration with edge-forming. If you're routing the perimeter of a workpiece, follow the conventional (counterclockwise) feed direction (see page 51), and start and finish the cut in the middle of an end-grain edge. Sweep into the cut initially to prevent burning (see Tip: A Sweeping Start, page 55). The objective with this technique is to remove any tearout that occurs on the end-grain cut when you make the subsequent long-grain cut. If you're routing only one edge, clamp a scrap piece to the work at the finish of the cut. This prevents tearout and keeps you from accidentally cutting into the adjacent edge.

When edging three sides of a piece, begin with a sweeping cut in the end grain. Complete the end with a climb cut. Edge the long-grain side. Edge the second cross-grain side using a backer board (above right).

The bane of bearings: As a guide system, the main drawback of a bearing is that it transfers any defects in the workpiece (or template) edge to the surface of the cut. There are three ways to deal with this. The most obvious solution is to joint or re-saw the edge of the workpiece before routing to provide a perfectly smooth surface for the bearing. Another solution is to use an edge guide. With this method, set the guide just inside of the bearing so the guide controls the cut instead of the bearing. The guide will bridge minor defects in the workpiece edge for a smoother cut. A third option is to make the cut on the router table using a fence.

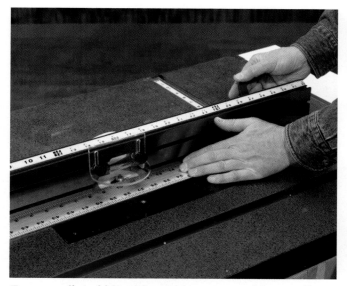

To use a piloted bit with a table router and fence, align the bearing with the fence, using a straightedge.

Create different profiles with the same bit by adjusting the bit depth or running the bearing along a template mounted beneath the workpiece.

Using piloted bits on the router table: You can use almost any type of edge-forming bit on the router table, with or without a fence. When using a fence, adjust it so it's flush with the bit's bearing; a straightedge helps to make the adjustment. If the workpiece edge is rough, set the fence slightly past the bearing so that the fence guides the cut. Contoured work is done without the fence, using a starting pin to stabilize the stock when starting the cut (see Routing without a fence, page 73).

Edge-forming with a template: This technique is used for shaping the entire edge of a workpiece. For example, to make a full-thickness roundover, cut a template to match the exact dimensions of the original workpiece. The bearing rides along the template below the work. Instead of a full-size template, you can also rout one edge at a time using a narrow strip of template material set flush to the workpiece edge. Templates also allow you to cut stock that's too thin to support a guide bearing.

A template below a thin workpiece supports the bearing and allows you to vary the profile.

Custom molding details: Household trimwork and architectural moldings that you buy at a lumberyard or home center are factory-cut on a large stationary tool called a shaper. Like a router, the shaper is a rotary tool with profiled cutters, but its power base is designed for production work and can handle much larger workpieces and more complex profiles than a router. A router table acts somewhat like a

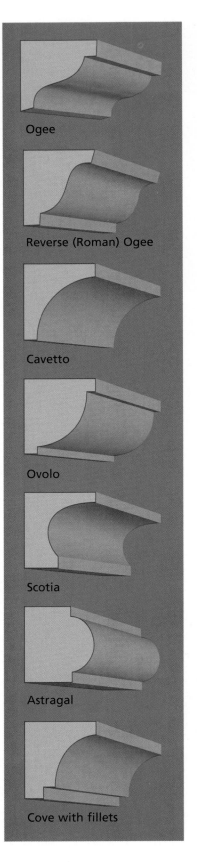

Ogee

Reverse (Roman) Ogee

Cavetto

Ovolo

Scotia

Astragal

Cove with fillets

shaper but with limited capabilities. For large jobs, have the work custom-milled by a professional shop.

With that said, you can make a lot of custom molding details with a router table and decorative profile bits. The chart at left shows some classical Greek and Roman molding details. You can decorate a piece of trim with a single detail or use them as building blocks to create more complex profiles. Another option is to use a specialty molding bit that cuts the desired profile in a single pass.

Rabbeting

A rabbet is a continuous, right-angle notch cut into the edge of a board. Rabbets are used to set panels flush into the backs of frames, for corner joints of drawer boxes and simple cases, and as a decorative detail. Using a hand-held router, you can cut a rabbet with a piloted rabbeting bit or a straight bit and edge guide. On a router table, use a straight bit with a fence or a piloted bit with or without a fence.

Rabbeting with a hand-held router: The most basic rabbeting technique calls for a hand-held router and a piloted rabbeting bit. The rabbet's width is set by the bit bearing, while the depth is set by you. Common rabbeting bits cut ¼", ⅜", or ½" rabbets. However, you can change the bearing to yield a different cutting width or buy a rabbeting bit set (see Bit Bearings, page 33, and Buying Bit Sets, page 30). To cut a rabbet wider than your bit will allow, you have to use a setup with a straight bit. Cut deeper rabbets by making successively deeper passes with a piloted or straight bit.

Rabbeting with a straight bit requires an edge guide, straightedge, or right-angle jig. The rabbet depth is set by the cutting depth of the bit. The width is determined by the placement of the guide or jig, so the rabbet can be as wide as you need. Tearout is a concern for any rabbet cut because you're cutting two surfaces that are vulnerable to splintering and chipping. Usually, the best way to minimize tearout is to make a narrow initial cut, or score, followed by a full-width final cut. This works because a narrower pass cuts a more gradual angle at the leading cutter edge. If you're still tearing out using a conventional feed, try a climb cut for the scoring pass, then a conventional feed for the final pass. Using a bit that's at least twice as big as the rabbet width (½"-diameter bit for a ¼" rabbet, for example) also helps reduce tearout.

Rabbeting on the router table: Rabbeting on a router table offers the usual advantages over hand-held routing: less telegraphing of defects from the stock edge (when using a fence), ease of working small or narrow stock, and no risk of ruining the cut due to a tipped router. Always use a fence for straight work. For curved workpieces you can omit the fence and use a bearing-guided bit and starting pin.

With a standard fence setup, use a straight, spiral, or piloted rabbeting bit. For straight or spiral bits, adjust the fence to the desired rabbet width, and adjust the bit height to equal the depth of cut. When using a rabbeting bit, set the fence even with the bit's bearing, or beyond the bearing to make a more narrow cut. Note: Never trap the work under the bit by cutting into the top side—bowed stock or lifting during the cut will ruin the cut and can break the bit.

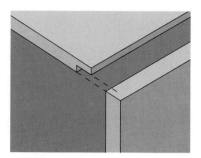

Rabbet joint

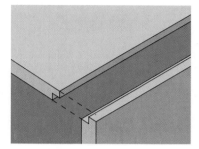

Double rabbet

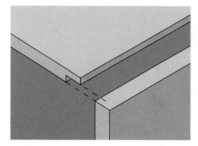

Overlap rabbet

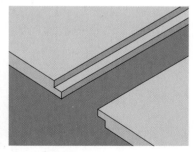

Shiplap rabbet

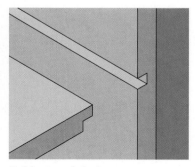

Rabbet and dado

Cut wide rabbets with a straight bit and right-angle jig.

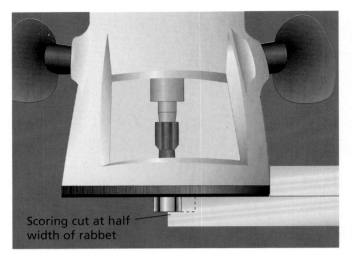

Scoring cut at half width of rabbet

To reduce tearout when making a rabbet cut, limit the first cut to ½ the diameter of the bit.

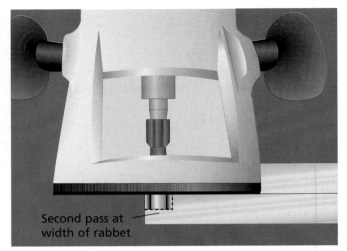

Second pass at width of rabbet

Then, move the edge guide and make a second pass to complete the rabbet.

Making a stopped rabbet: Stopped rabbets run short of one or both ends of a workpiece and are good for hiding the edges of panels and construction joints. Cut them like standard rabbets, but use stop blocks to index the ends of the cut. With a hand-held router, clamp blocks across the work (perpendicular to the rabbet), allowing for the distance between the edge of the subbase and the bit. Initiate the cut by pivoting the workpiece into the spinning bit—make a sweeping cut (see Tip: A Sweeping Start, page 55) with a conventional feed until you reach the far stop block. Then come back and sweep into a climb cut to finish up the remaining few inches of the rabbet. On a router table, set up the cut with marks and stop blocks as described in Making stopped cuts, on page 74.

Working with Plastic Laminate

Any hand-held router will work for the basic operations of rough-cutting and trimming laminate, but if you own a trim router, this is the time to use it. Laminate is what trim routers are made for. They're light and easy to maneuver around corners, and their small bases let you cut close into corners to minimize hand work. If you're building countertops, check out the laminate accessories available from your trim router's manufacturer.

Never raise the bit to cut into the top side of a board. This can trap the stock under the bit, causing accidents.

The basic procedure for installing laminate involves cutting the sheet stock to size, gluing the laminate to the substrate with contact cement, then trimming the edges flush. It's easy to make a laminate job look professional, because the router takes care of the accuracy. But be aware that mistakes can be costly. Contact cement is totally unforgiving once it's stuck; and gouged, chipped, or scratched laminate cannot be repaired.

You can buy laminate from lumberyards and home centers or directly from a manufacturer's dealer. Whenever possible, avoid seams by buying a sheet big enough to cover the entire job. To prevent the substrate from warping, laminate both sides of any

For stopped rabbets, clamp stop blocks to the router table fence, and rotate the workpiece into the bit. Initiate the cut about 1" from the front rabbet mark.

Create a decorative edge by applying laminate over a hardwood edge strip, then routing a cove profile.

piece that isn't well supported and fastened to a structure below. You can save money by covering the bottom face with a backer, or balancing, sheet—a thinner, more economical version of regular laminate.

Laminate bits: Most manufacturers offer an assortment of bits for working laminate. Use only carbide-tipped or solid-carbide bits. Steel bits will dull quickly on the hard plastic. Any flush-trimming, bearing-guided straight bit will make the basic cuts and work well for cutting stock pieces to size. If you buy one specifically for laminate work, choose a short cutter for greater rigidity. Solid-carbide laminate trimming bits with solid pilots are also popular. When using these, lubricate the bit or substrate with wax or petroleum jelly to prevent marring of the laminate. The most common specialty laminate bit is the bevel trimmer, which is available in a variety of bevel angles. Also common are three-flute bits for an ultra-smooth finish.

Rough-cutting the laminate: What makes laminate work so easy is that you cut the workpieces large so they overhang the substrate by ¼" or so on all sides. Once the stock is glued in place, the trimming cleans up the edges. Use a handheld mid-size or trim router to cut laminate stock to size. If it seems to stress your trim router, make the rough cuts with a mid-size, and use the smaller tool for the trimming work.

Mark the cuts on the stock, then lay it over a flat, wide straightedge panel of MDF, plywood, or other sheet goods. Make sure the panel's working edge is straight and without voids or defects (these will transfer to the cut). Clamp the stock down with the cutting marks aligned with the straightedge. Make the cut using a bearing-guided, flush-trimming bit, letting the bearing ride along the straightedge. Use the conventional, left-to-right feed direction. The waste should fall onto a work surface; don't let it hang down over an edge or it can snap off as you near the end of the cut.

Laminate cutters include (from top to bottom) laminate kit with flush and beveled cutters and two bearings, flush-trimming straight bit with bearing, bevel-cutting bit with bearing, solid-carbide single-flute bevel trimmer and solid-carbide single-flute flush trimmer.

When cutting laminate, clamp the stock over the straight-edge so the waste falls onto the work surface. Be careful not to crack or scratch the laminate if using metal clamps. Use a guided bit to make the cut.

Applying the laminate: Apply an even layer of contact cement to the back of the laminate and the substrate surface, using a paint roller. Let the cement dry to tackiness, as directed by the manufacturer. Once the two surfaces touch, they're stuck for good, so be careful when laying down the laminate. Note: If you're laminating two adjacent surfaces, see Edge Options, page 85, to determine the proper application sequence.

With large sheets, use a helper and lay clean wooden shims or dowels spaced evenly over the substrate. Place the laminate so it overhangs the substrate evenly on all sides (the overhang doesn't have to be exact). Starting at one end, press the laminate onto the substrate, then roll it out with a rubber J-roller to create a strong bond and remove air bubbles. Remove the shims one at a time as you work toward the other end. Roll the surface thoroughly. You can start trimming immediately, as there's no additional curing or drying time for contact cement.

Trimming the laminate: Set the depth of the trimming bit so the bottom of the cutters are about $\frac{1}{16}$" below the laminate. Make sure the bit is free of glue residue and that the bearing rolls freely; a squirt of WD40 helps remove glue. Check the substrate edge that the bearing will ride against—any dips, bumps, or voids here will show up in the cut. Trim the edge using a conventional feed and keeping the router's base flat at all times. If you want to bevel an edge, trim

Use wood shims to keep the cemented surfaces from making contact. Remove the shims one at a time and roll each section with a J-roller to eliminate air bubbles.

EDGE OPTIONS

There a many ways to dress up a countertop or table edge. Here are a few of the most popular styles.

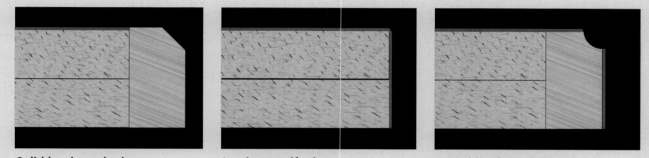

Solid hardwood edge **Laminate self edge** **Coved hardwood edge**

it flush first with a straight bit, then use a beveling bit for the final pass. This yields a smoother finished edge.

The last step in laminate work is a quick buff with a fine, flat file. This removes the white markings left by the router bit and slightly rounds over the sharp edge, which can cut you if left raw. Hold the file with two hands and move it parallel with the edge. One to three light passes is all it should take to produce a clean, dark edge that's slightly dulled for safety. If you're overlapping one laminate edge over another, there's no need to file the first (lower) piece.

The final step in a custom laminate job is filing the edges to soften and clean the profile.

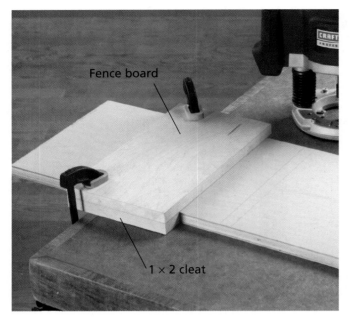

Fence board

1 × 2 cleat

A right-angle jig can easily be shop made. Make sure the cleat (the overhanging lip) is perfectly square to the fence board edge.

Straight-line Guide Routing

The principal functions of straight-line guide routing are cutting dadoes and grooves and trimming and squaring stock. All of this work is made possible with simple shop-made jigs, one-piece straightedges, or commercial edge guides, or with the fence on a router table. Dadoes and grooves are square channels cut into the stock. Technically, a dado runs against the grain, and a groove runs with the grain, but both are made using the same techniques and setups. Dadoes and basic grooves primarily are joinery cuts but can be used for aesthetic effects. The term grooving also applies to decorative, straight-line details applied to the surface of stock, and may be with or against the grain.

For hand-held routing, the right jig makes the work easy. These shop-made jigs are great for dadoes, grooves, squaring stock, and other straight-line operations. Make them out of any material you like. Of the jigs you use more often, you'll probably end up building a few versions to accommodate different situations and stock sizes.

Note: The principal behind most straight-line jigs (as well as all straightedge work) is to provide a clean edge for guiding the router's subbase. It follows that if the subbase is not concentric to the bit (that is, the distance between the bit and the subbase's outer edge varies depending on the position of the router), you may get inconsistent results with your cuts. One way to correct this is to keep the router in the same position relative to the jig every time you make a pass. A better solution is to center the subbase over the collet so the results will be the same regardless of the router's orientation (see Centering the Subbase,

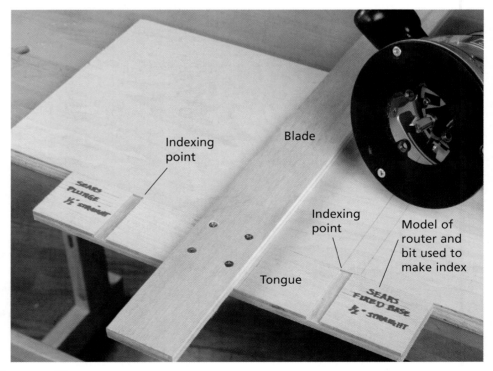

Indexing point

Blade

Indexing point

Model of router and bit used to make index

Tongue

Routing grooves through the crossbar of a T-square creates an indexing cut. Make note of which bit was used, and which router, if you have more than one.

page 88). However, because subbases are not always perfectly round, it's best to be able to use both solutions.

Right-angle jig: This simple jig guides cuts that are perpendicular to the workpiece edge. Use it for dadoes and cleaning up or squaring the ends of stock. Glue and screw a jointed 1 × 2 cleat to the underside of a flat fence board that has at least one straight edge. The cleat must be perfectly square (90 degrees) to the straight fence edge. The jig is even more useful if both fence edges are straight and square to the cleat.

T-square: A variation of the right-angle jig, the T-square provides an indexing point that shows you exactly where the cut will be. It's also easy to make in different sizes. Start with a long, straight blade piece and a shorter, straight tongue piece. Glue and screw them together at a right angle to form a "T"; extend the blade past the tongue to provide an overhang to help when starting cuts.

To make the indexing point, clamp the T-square to a scrap board, then set up your router with the straight bit you'll most likely use with the square. Rout a groove through the tongue piece and into the scrap. When you make real cuts using the same router and bit, align the inside edge of the groove with the cut mark. Note the model of router and bit on the jig. If desired, make another indexing groove on the other side of the tongue, using a different bit or router. Note those particulars, as well.

Saddle dado jig: The saddle jig has two fences that trap the router's base and allow you to cut dadoes wider than the bit diameter without readjusting the jig. Build the jig with two straight fence pieces (long enough to span the widest stock you're likely to use) and two cleats (long enough to accommodate the two fences, the router's subbase, and extra lateral room that determines the dado width).

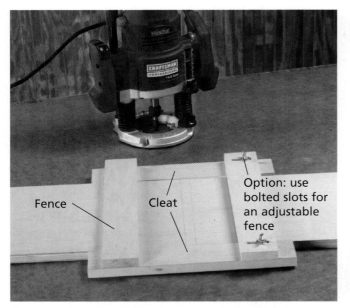

A saddle dado jig allows for easy and consistent repeatability of dado cuts that are wider than the bit diameter.

A square, off-center subbase makes it easy to do incremental cuts with only one straightedge setup.

CENTERING THE SUBBASE

Centering the subbase of your router helps ensure accuracy when using straight-line jigs, straight-edges, and template guides. With some routers, you can do this using the router's collet; for others, a centering gauge accessory is the way to go. Using the collet method, unplug the tool and loosen the subbase mounting screws just enough to allow movement. Adjust the depth setting until the collet engages the center hole in the subbase, then lock down the motor. Tighten the mounting screws making sure the subbase is centered over the collet.

This subbase can be centered from the collet.

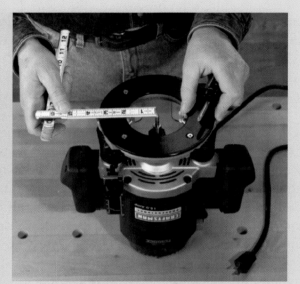

Loosen screws in a standard subbase and measure from four sides to center the subbase.

Glue and screw the cleats to the fences to form a perfectly square assembly. As a variation, you can mill slots into one of the fences and use bolts run through the cleats to make the fence adjustable. To use the jig, clamp it to the workpiece so one of the cleats is flush against the workpiece edge.

Off-center subbase: This shop-made subbase has four flat sides, each with a different offset from the base edge to the bit. It allows you to make multiple incremental cuts with one edge setting. Also, since you're aligning a straight base edge against a straight fence, it eliminates the concentricity problems that plague round subbases.

Start with a blank of plywood, MDF, or acrylic. Remove the factory subbase from your router and mount the router base directly to the blank. Make a center hole by loading a straight bit and plunging it down into the blank. Remove the router and mark each of the four sides by measuring from the center hole. Make one edge a control, and measure the remaining three sides based on their deviation from the control. For example: Side 1 = control, Side 2 = control + $\frac{1}{16}$"; Side 3 = control + $\frac{1}{8}$"; Side 4 = control + $\frac{3}{16}$".

Cut each side at its mark and note the deviations on the jig. You can make the center hole as large as needed to accommodate other bits.

PERFECTING PLYWOOD

Plywood is a great material for shelf systems and cabinet boxes, but cutting dadoes for the shelves brings up two common problems: tearout and improper bit sizing. Prevent the thin outer veneers on plywood from tearing out by scoring both sides of the dado with a utility knife. And when it comes to choosing a bit, make sure the thickness of your plywood shelves matches the bit diameter. Sometimes plywood actually measures a little thicker or thinner than its labeled dimension. Many bit manufacturers offer dado and straight bits in odd sizes, such as $^{23}\!/_{32}$" and $^{49}\!/_{64}$", to match different plywood sizes.

Using Commercial Edge Guides

Commercial edge guides have adjustable fences that ride along the workpiece edge to control the cut. Most types mount directly to the router's base by means of two steel rods. Router manufacturers make edge guides to fit their own routers, and there are several aftermarket guides available.

Since they provide their own fence, edge guides are best for making long grooves close to the workpiece edge; the length of the sliding rods limits how far the guide can make an interior cut. You can also set them up to cut mortises, and some fences are designed to follow curved work. When buying an edge guide, look for stiff rods that hold the fence firmly and resist chatter during cuts. Adjustability is another key feature. Some guides have screw-drive adjustment mechanisms for precise movement.

Edge guides are available for most router models.

Use the conventional feed direction when routing with edge guides, so the working forces of the bit will help hold the fence against the workpiece edge.

When making stopped grooves, as with this classical flute design, use stop blocks to keep the ends of the grooves even.

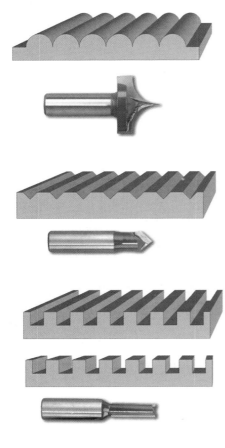

Decorative grooving options are endless. Three common styles are beading made with a point-cutting roundover bit; V-grooves made with a V-groove or veining bit; and dentil molding made by dadoing a board with a straight bit.

Flutes & other decorative grooving: Decorative grooves are controlled cuts made with a non-piloted bit. Because they typically run parallel to a board's long edges, they're easiest to make with a hand-held router and edge guide or on the router table. Stopped grooves, however, require precise plunging to initiate the cut and quick retraction of the bit at the end, so are best made with a hand-held plunge router. Classic surface treatments, like fluting and beading, take some time to set up, but the general techniques are simple and straightforward.

Start by laying out the cuts across the face of the stock. Work outward from the center if the design is symmetrical. Mark the centerpoint and outer edges of each cut to ensure even spacing and help with adjusting the fence. For router table work, also mark one end of the stock as a reference for setting the fence. With the layout complete and the bit loaded, set the edge guide or table fence so the bit is centered over the outermost groove. With a symmetrical design, you can rout the corresponding grooves on both sides before changing the fence setting.

Cutting circles & ellipses: No workshop tool cuts circles as cleanly or efficiently as a router. And the setup couldn't be simpler. This is a job for a hand-held router—preferably a plunge router, which allows you to plunge safely into the work to initiate the cut. If you don't own a commercial circle jig, make a trammel jig out of ¼" plywood or hardboard.

Cut the trammel board a little wider than your router's base and several inches longer than the radius of the circle you want to make. Cut a hole for the bit, then mount the router base directly (without its subbase) to one end of the trammel, using countersunk bolts driven up through the trammel's underside. Load the bit you'll use for the cut. Measure straight out from the

A trammel jig mounts to the router base. A nail or screw anchors the trammel at the circle's centerpoint as you pivot around the workpiece.

inside edge of the cutter and mark the circle's radius on the trammel; this is the pivot point.

To cut the circle, drive a small nail through the pivot point and into the stock. Set the bit depth at about ⅛". Plunge the router into the work and feed it counterclockwise to complete the first pass. (With a fixed-base router, you'll have to tilt the router and carefully plunge the spinning bit into the work to start the cut.) Make successively deeper cuts until the circle is complete.

Cutting ovals and elliptical arcs works much the same as making circles but requires special jigs.

Commercial jigs for cutting circles and ellipses are also available.

MAKING CROSSHAIRS ON A DISK

You've just cut a circle and need crosshair marks for centering parts on the disk. Here's how you do it: Use a framing square to draw a straight line through the disk's centerpoint. Align one leg of the square with the line so the square's corner is at the centerpoint. Draw a line along the perpendicular leg of the square. Extend the second line through the centerpoint and across the disk's face.

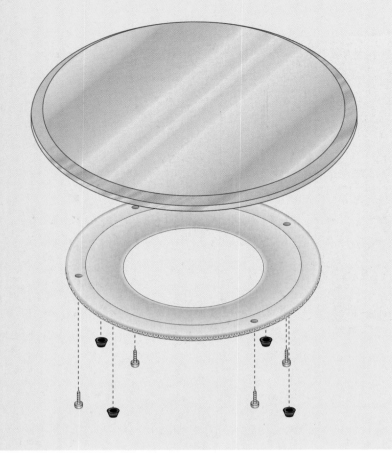

Project: Tabletop Lazy Susan

This simple project is easy to customize to suit your table size and room decor. It can even be made for an outdoor table. The design includes only two main parts: a wood top and a bearing plate. You can make the top with plywood, MDF, or a glued-up plank of oak, pine, or other solid wood. The one requirement is that the top stays flat—warpage causes the bearing to bind and makes for rough travel.

The bearing plate itself is a fairly common hardware item made for lazy Susan cabinets, available at home centers, lumberyards, and woodworking suppliers. It has two metal rings that spin on ball bearings. Holes in the rings allow you to fasten the plate between two surfaces by means of an access hole. (To sandwich the plate between two surfaces, you drill through the lower surface and screw into the upper surface via the access hole.)

When determining the best size for your lazy Susan, set your table as though for a typical meal, to see how much free space is in the center. You might be surprised by how small your final design will be. For an average-size table, a 16"-diameter Susan is a good size to start with.

MATERIALS

- ⅝" or ¾" plywood, MDF, or solid-wood top stock
- Bearing plate
- Screws (must be shorter than thickness of top)
- Finishing materials
- Stick-on felt furniture pads or rubber feet

PROJECT: LAZY SUSAN

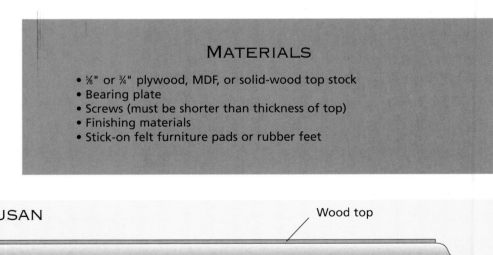
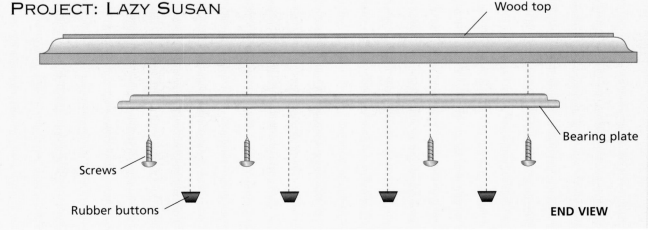

Wood top

Bearing plate

Screws

Rubber buttons

END VIEW

How to Make the Lazy Susan

Step 1. Cut the top using the trammel technique shown on page 91 or a commercial circle jig. Work with the stock face-down, so as not to mar the top surface with the hole made by the pivot nail. Once the disk is cut, you can form the edges as you like. An ogee or similar detail adds a traditional look, for example. Or you might want to match the edge of your table. A plywood top with exposed edges usually looks best with a simple roundover. Another option is to leave the edge with a square cut and wrap it with wood veneer tape.

Step 2. Center the bearing plate over the bottom face of the top, using crosshair lines or by measuring for an equal margin along the perimeter. The smaller ring of the bearing plate (the ring without the access hole) goes against the top. Rotate the larger plate ring to line up the access hole with the screw holes in the smaller ring. There may be several sets of screw holes—use only one set so that the screws placement is symmetrical. Drill pilot holes for the screws but do not install the bearing.

Step 3. Sand and finish the top as desired, then install the bearing plate. Once the screws are snugged down, you may have to adjust them slightly to prevent binding of the bearing. Add stick-on felt pads or rubber feet arranged evenly around the bottom of the bearing plate. These provide some friction and prevent scratches to the table.

Note: In the future, if the top warps and hinders the bearing's travel, try using a flexible joint: remove the bearing and add dabs of caulk around the upper plate ring, then refasten the bearing, leaving the screws a little loose. Once dry, the caulk will help hold the top firmly and should reduce the binding caused by warpage.

VARIATION: An Outdoor Lazy Susan

If your lazy Susan will be left outdoors on a patio table, just make sure the top is adequately sealed to protect it from water and sun damage. Most bearing plates are made with rust-protected materials, but you'll want to raise it up with rubber feet to keep it out of pooling water. If your table has an umbrella, drill a center hole through the top as part of Step 1.

Cut the circle to size, then trim the edge.

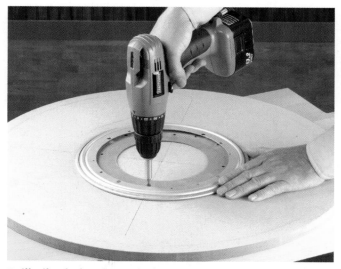
Drill pilot holes through the access hole in bearing plate.

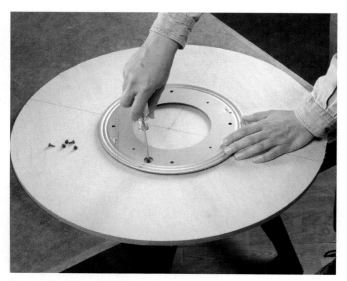
Screw the bearing plate onto the base.

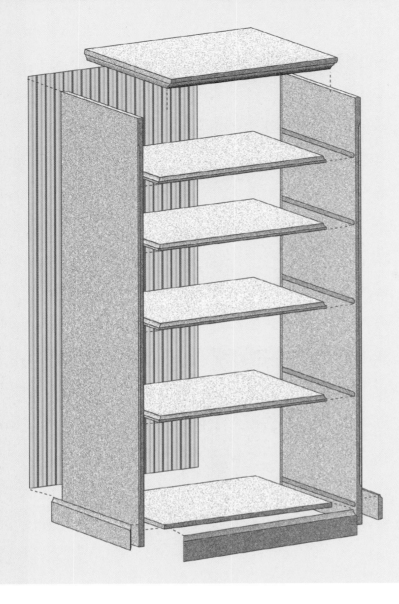

Project: Classic Bookcase

With its clean lines and traditional styling, this bookcase demonstrates how basic router cuts can add character to an ordinary functional piece. The box, or carcase, of the bookcase uses dado and rabbet joinery for strength and a quality appearance and is dressed up with a molded baseboard and ornamental top piece. Additional edge-forming cuts add detail to the bookcase sides and shelf edges. All of these decorative elements can be made with standard router bits, and you can easily adapt the bookcase design to suit your needs.

You can build the project as shown from a single 4 × 8-ft. sheet of ¾" MDF and a 2 × 6-ft. sheet of ¼" plywood or paneling board. This is the cheapest way to go and will yield the best finish for a painted bookcase. Of course, plywood and solid lumber also are good materials; however, the layered edges of plywood don't edge-form as well as MDF or solid wood and may show lines through paint.

How to Build the Classic Bookcase

Step 1. Cut all parts except the back panel to size, using a table saw or circular saw and straightedge guide. Make sure all of the shelves are exactly the same length. Lay out the dadoes

MATERIALS

- 4 × 8-ft. sheet of ¾" MDF
- 2 × 6-ft. sheet of ¼" plywood or paneling board (with beadboard grooves optional)
- Wood glue
- 2" coarse-thread drywall screws
- Finishing materials
- Brads
- Finish nails

CUTTING LIST

2 SIDES @ ¾ × 11½ × 68½"
1 BOTTOM SHELF @ ¾ × 11½ × 23"
4 SHELVES @ ¾ × 11 × 23"
1 SUBTOP @ ¾ × 12¼ × 25½"
1 TOP @ ¾ × 12¾ × 26½"
1 BASEBOARD @ ¾ × 4 × 54" (cut lengths to fit)
1 BACK PANEL @ ¼ × 2¼ × 65" (cut to fit)

PROJECT: CLASSIC BOOKCASE

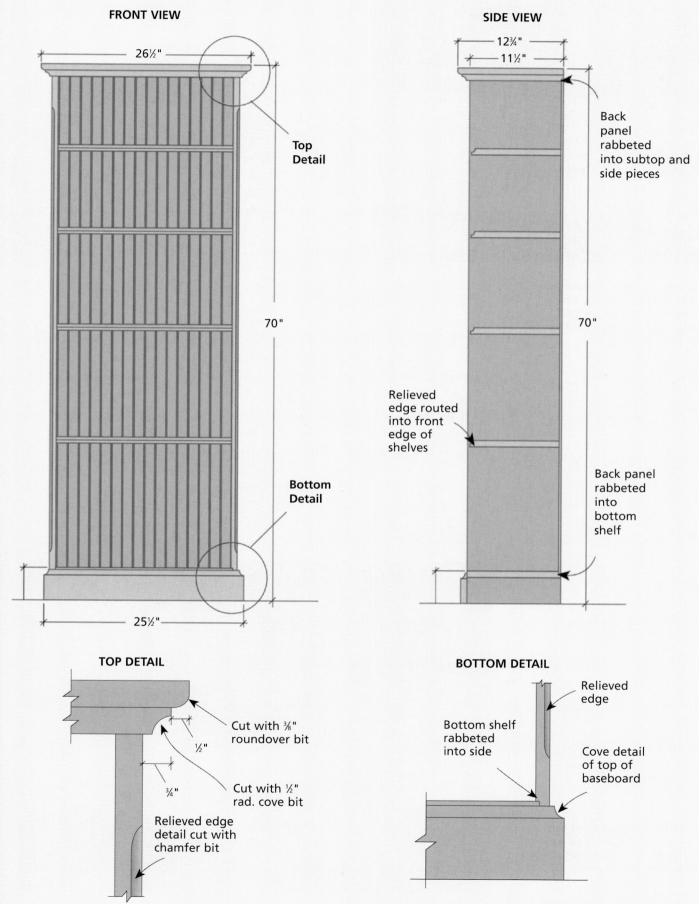

FRONT VIEW

26½"

Top Detail

70"

Bottom Detail

25½"

SIDE VIEW

12¾"

11½"

Back panel rabbeted into subtop and side pieces

70"

Relieved edge routed into front edge of shelves

Back panel rabbeted into bottom shelf

TOP DETAIL

Cut with ⅜" roundover bit

½"

¾"

Cut with ½" rad. cove bit

Relieved edge detail cut with chamfer bit

BOTTOM DETAIL

Relieved edge

Bottom shelf rabbeted into side

Cove detail of top of baseboard

Lay out the shelf dadoes on side pieces. Butt the back edges of the sides together, align the pieces, and mark the dados.

on both side pieces. Check the thickness of the shelves to make sure the dadoes will provide a snug fit (dadoes cut with a ¾" bit might be too wide). The bottom shelf gets a ¼"-deep through dado with its top edge 4¼" from the bottom end of each side. The remaining four shelves fit into ¼"-deep stopped dadoes that run through the back edge and stop ¾" from the front edges of the sides. Set the shelf spacing as desired. Cut the dadoes with a straight bit and straight-line jig. Square off the rounded ends of the stopped dadoes with a sharp chisel.

Step 2. Rabbet the back edges of the sides, subtop, and bottom shelf to receive the back panel. This is easiest to do on a router table, using a straight bit and fence set to cut a ⅜"-wide × ¼"-deep rabbet. Rabbet the bottom shelf and sides along their entire length (through rabbets). On the subtop, stop the rabbet 1⅛" from each end (stopped rabbet), then square it with a chisel.

Step 3. Cut ¼ × ½" notches in the front corners of the four regular shelves, so the shelves will fit into the stopped dadoes and the front corners will butt tightly against the faces of the sides.

Step 4. Mill decorative edges into the bookcase parts as desired. In the project shown, the top has a roundover on the front and side edges, and the subtop has a cove on the same edges. The four regular shelves have a slightly coved front edge. The baseboard is also coved. Finally, the outside corners of the sides have a 45-degree relief detail cut with a chamfer bit.

Step 5. Dry-assemble the sides, shelves, and subtop, clamping the carcase

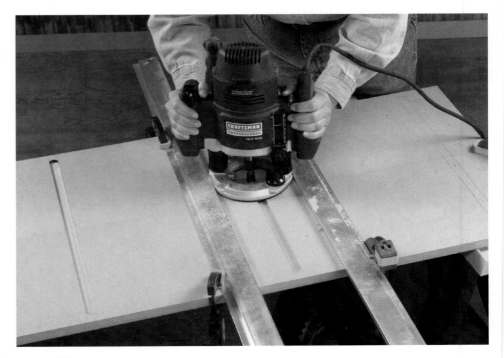

Mill the stopped shelf dados on both side pieces at the same time to make sure they are perfectly aligned.

Rout decorative edging as desired. Here, we routed camfers on the outside front edges of the sides.

To ensure that the bookcase is square, measure the diagonals. If both diagonals are equal, the case is square.

together to see how everything fits. Measure the diagonals to make sure the assembly is square, then measure and cut the back panel to fit. If you plan to paint the bookcase, cut the back panel slightly smaller than the rabbeted cavity to leave some room for the paint. Disassemble the carcase.

Step 6. Lightly sand all of the pieces. Apply glue to all mating surfaces, and assemble and clamp the carcase. Do not install the back panel in this step. Fasten through the sides into the shelf ends, and through the subtop into the side ends, with screws driven through counterbored pilot holes. Glue the top to the subtop and clamp the pieces well so the top is flat. Confirm that the carcase is square, then let the glue dry.

Install the mitered baseboards.

Step 7. Fill the screw holes along the sides with wood putty and sand the areas smooth. Finish the carcase, back panel, and baseboard as desired. Install the back panel and fasten it to the sides, shelves, and subtop with brads. Cut the baseboard to fit along the front and sides of the bookcase, mitering the joints at the corners. Install the baseboard with glue and finish nails. (Note: You might want to add the baseboard after setting the bookcase in its permanent place, to hide any gaps along the floor.)

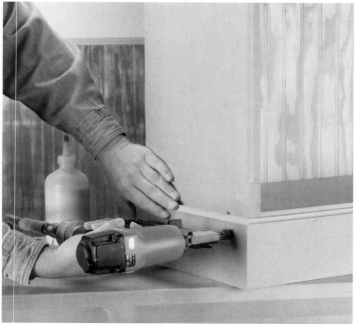

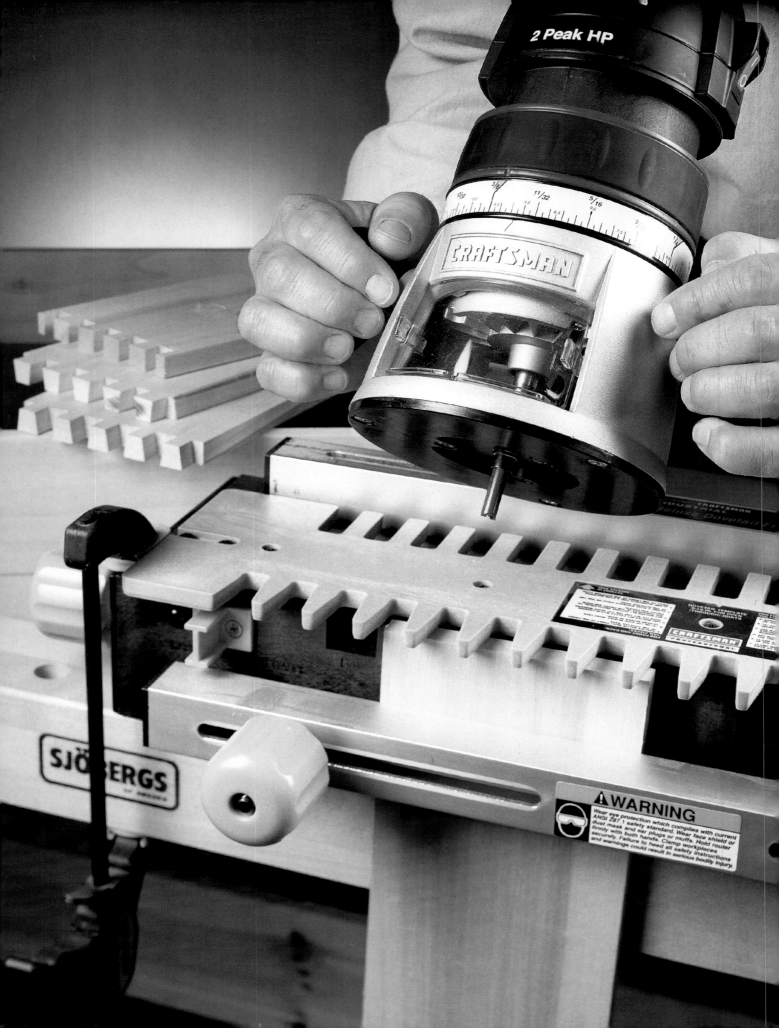

Chapter 6
ROUTER JOINERY

A router makes classic woodworking joints much less intimidating. Several traditional joints, including mortise-and-tenon, box, and lap joints, are made with nothing more than a straight bit and a simple shop-made jig. You can make flawless dovetails using a commercial template or build custom frame-and-panel doors with the help of a few edge-forming bits. The key to success is in the setup. Fine-tuning your adjustments and making test cuts is what joinery is all about. But just as important is using good, straight stock of uniform thickness. Without it, you'll spend all your time setting up the cuts and your joints still won't fit well.

Mortise & Tenon Joints

The mortise-and-tenon is an essential frame joint found in everything from timber barns to fine furniture. Secured with glue, the joint is one of the strongest wood connections possible. It resists twisting, racking, and pulling apart, making it ideal for cabinet doors and table frames. If desired, the connection can be completely invisible in the finished product. The router does a good job of cutting both the mortise (the slot) and the tenon (the tongue that fits into the mortise).

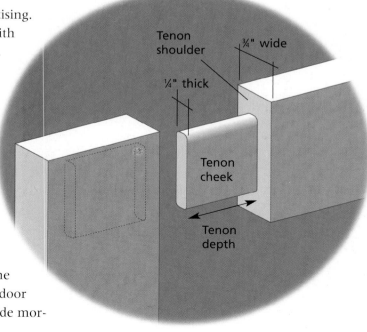

Blind mortise-and-tenon joint

A plunge router is the best and safest tool for mortising. Tenons can be cut in several different ways, with fixed-base, plunge, or table-mounted routers. Hand-held operations generally require a jig that holds the workpiece vertically while the router cuts around the end to form the tenon. A simpler method—using the router table—is shown here.

In most cases, it's easiest to cut the mortises first, then cut the tenons to fit the mortises. This allows you to trim away the tenon gradually and "sneak up" on a tight-fitting joint. Use a plunge-cutting straight or spiral bit for mortising. Size the mortise so it's about ⅓ the thickness of the stock that will receive the tenon. For example, a door frame with ¾"-thick rails should have ¼"- or ⁵⁄₁₆"-wide mortises cut into the stiles.

Mark the outline of the mortise on the workpiece.

Use the mortise outline to set up the edge guide and stop blocks. Side supports ensure stability while making the cut.

To cut a mortise wider than the bit diameter, use a saddle jig or two straightedges to guide the cut.

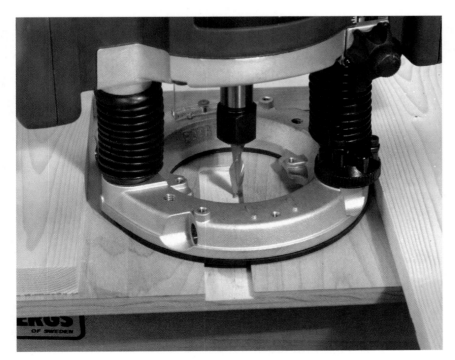

Mortise cutting with edge guide: A commercial edge guide on a plunge router makes for an easy mortising setup (if you don't have an edge guide, use a fixed straightedge or fence to guide the router base). Start by marking the center of the mortise on the workpiece, then measure from the centerline and mark the mortise's outer edges. Mark the ends of the mortise. If you're working with narrow stock, clamp extra pieces to either side of the workpiece to support the router's base. Load the bit and set the plunge depth to equal the full depth of the mortise. Place the router on the work and sight the bit against the pencil marks to set the guide fence. Also set up stop blocks that will contact the router base at the ends of the cut. Make the cut incrementally with ⅛" passes, cutting the full length of the mortise with each pass. Keep the router upright and the guide fence tight to the work throughout the operation, removing waste chips with a vacuum or air hose as needed.

Mortise cutting with jig: An alternative to mortising with an edge guide is to use a slotted jig. One design works with a template guide (see page 125) to control the router; another uses stop blocks fixed to the jig.

To make the template-guide jig, fasten a straight fence to the underside of a ¼" MDF or hardboard base. On the router table, cut a slot through the base that

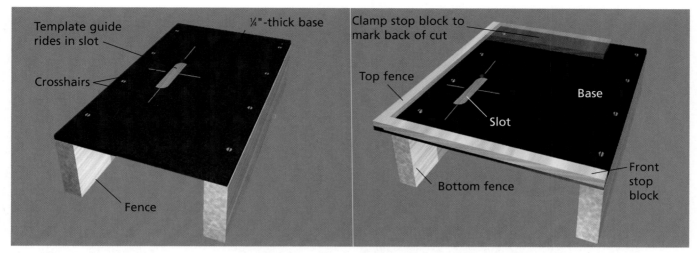

Template guide rides in slot

Crosshairs

¼"-thick base

Fence

Clamp stop block to mark back of cut

Top fence

Slot

Base

Bottom fence

Front stop block

Mortising jig for use with a template guide (above left). Mortising jig for use with mortising bits (above right).

matches the outside diameter of your template guide. The length of the slot equals the mortise length plus 2 times the offset of the template guide to the bit. Locate the slot so the jig can be centered on the thickest stock you're likely to use. Add crosshairs marking the center of the slot to help position the jig. For thinner stock, place shims between the fence and workpiece.

The stop-block jig has a fence on the bottom side of its base and one on the top side. Attach these so they are parallel to each other. Also attach a front stop block to the top side, perpendicular to the fences. Using the top fence and stop block to guide your hand-held router, cut the slot using your mortising bit. The front end of the slot will always mark the front end of the mortise. To set up the jig, clamp it to the work (using shims if necessary to center the slot over the work), then clamp a stop block behind the router to mark the back end of the mortise.

Routing tenons: Making classic, four-sided tenons is easiest on the table router. All you need is a fence, a straight bit, and a push sled or miter gauge. Since you're cutting tenons to fit existing mortises, it's best to err on the side of making them too big, then nibble them down for a good fit. Use the mortises to test-fit each tenon, and make adjustments carefully—any change in the bit depth has a doubled effect because you always cut from both sides.

Mark the length of the tenon onto the stock: it should be ¹⁄₃₂" to ¹⁄₁₆" shorter than the mortise depth, to leave a little room for glue. Set the fence using the marks.

Use shims with the mortising jigs to center the workpiece in the slot.

If you cut numerous mortises of the same size in the same stock, create a permanent jig by screwing in stop blocks and spacers, rather than clamping them.

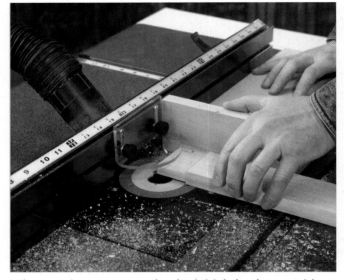

When cutting tenons, make the initial cheek cuts with the bit set at ⅛" depth. Use a sled or miter gauge to keep the work square.

Use the mortised workpiece to set the bit height for the final cheek cuts.

Adjust the bit height to cut about ⅛" for the initial pass. Make the cheek cuts using the push sled or block to keep the work square to the fence and back up the work to prevent tearout. Nibble away the end of the stock and work toward the fence with successive passes. Cut on both sides of the stock to keep the tenon centered. Re-set the bit height for the final passes, using the mortise as a gauge. Test-fit and re-cut as needed to achieve the proper thickness.

Mark the tenon for the width cuts, set the bit height, and make the cuts in light passes as with the cheek cuts. Because the bit guard must be removed for this cut, be very aware of your hand placement in relation to the bit. Complete the tenon by rounding over its square corners with a file. To protect the shoulders, file to within ⅛" of them, then clean up the rest with a chisel. The tenon should fit snugly in the mortise with no wiggle room, but should not require a lot of force or a hammer to seat it.

Cut the tenon to width, making light passes. Use an L-shaped push sled to support the work.

Use a file to slightly round the tenon, being careful not to mar the shoulder.

MORTISE & TENON VARIATIONS

Mortise-and-tenon joints come in a variety of styles for different situations. The common variations shown here are made using the same techniques as for the classic joint, with specific modifications as noted.

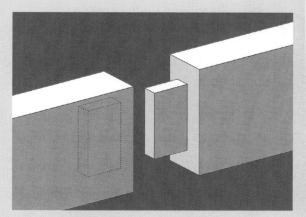

Square mortise: Mortise is squared at corners (with a chisel) to match tenon.

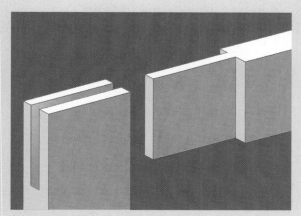

Open mortise: Mortise continues through end of stock. Often used where table aprons meet legs. Intersecting tenons can be mitered to increase length.

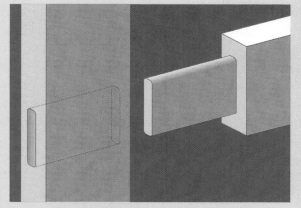

Through mortise: Mortise continues through back of stock. Used as decorative effect.

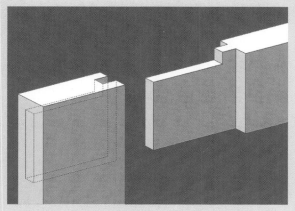

Haunched tenon: Haunch on outside edge of tenon prevents twisting. Commonly used in cabinet door construction.

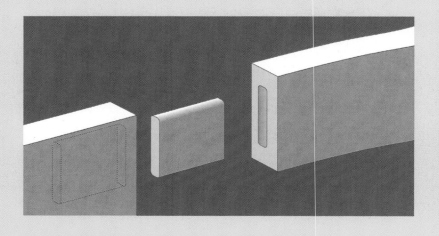

Loose tenon: Both mating pieces receive same-size mortise. Separate tenon glued inside. Good for hard-to-cut pieces or angles.

Lap Joints

The simplest of the frame joints, laps hold their own in terms of strength due to their broad, long-grain to long-grain gluing surfaces. They're great for a quick, strong connection where it's acceptable for the joint to show. A lap joint between contrasting wood members can be used for a decorative effect. Laps also make an effective connection with stock that is too thin for a mortise-and-tenon joint.

The lap joint used most commonly for frames is the half-lap, in which the ends of adjoining pieces are rabbeted to half their thickness, resulting in a flush fit. Laps can also be made at angles, can be located in the middle of pieces (cross-lap), or can consist of one uncut piece set into a notched piece (full lap). Basic lap joints are easy to cut with either a hand-held router and straight-line jig or on a router table.

Cutting a half-lap with a hand-held router: Mark the width of the stock onto the workpieces, then gang them together to make both cuts at once. Use a straight bit that makes a clean bottom cut. For end-laps, set up a right-angle jig so the fence will stop the router at the marks. Cut from the ends inward, making successive passes until reaching full depth of cut. Use test cuts to determine the proper bit depth for the final cut. If the lap is long, clamp a block to the workbench to support the router base. To cut a cross-lap joint, use two right-angle jigs (or straightedges) to trap the router base.

Cutting a half-lap on the router table: Load a straight bit and set the height at about ⅛". Mark the stock width onto the workpieces, then adjust the fence

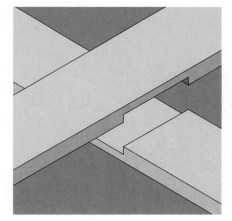

Square corner half-lap   Cross-lap joint   Angled full lap joint.

To cut cross-laps, use guides clamped to both sides to trap the router base.

When cutting square corner half-lap joints, gang the workpieces and cut from the ends inward.

so the outer edge of the bit will cut at the line. Cut both workpieces at once, using a sled or backer board if necessary. Cut from the ends of the stock, working inward until the pieces meet the fence. Re-cut at deeper bit settings until you reach full depth. If necessary, clean up the lap cheeks with a chisel.

HALVING THE WORKPIECE

Here's an easy way to find the correct bit depth for making half-lap joints. With each bit setting, make test cuts on both sides of the stock. When the two cuts meet, the bit is set to cut away exactly half of the stock.

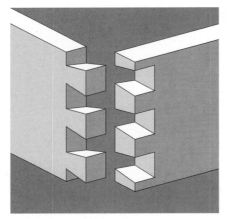

Through dovetail joint

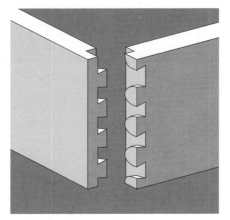

Half-blind dovetail joint

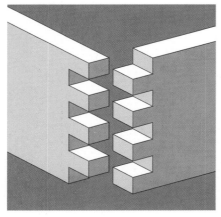

Box joint

Dovetail & Box Joints

Dovetail and box joints are traditional joints typically used for building box frames, such as drawer boxes and carcases. Their connections are made up of interlocking fingers (called tails and pins in dovetail joints) that yield an exceptionally strong joint with undeniable visual appeal. Dovetail joints in particular have been regarded by furniture makers for centuries as symbols of craftsmanship and quality construction. The best way to rout dovetails is with a hand-held router and a commercial dovetail jig. Box joints can be made using a special template on a dovetail jig or with a shop-made jig on the router table.

Types of dovetails: The two main styles of dovetail joints differ mostly in appearance. With a through dovetail, the tails and pins are visible in the assembled joint. With a half-blind dovetail, only the faces of the tails are visible. Half-blinds are used most commonly for drawer construction, because the pin board (always the front and back piece of the drawer box) retains an uncut outer face. Drawers also benefit from the mechanical connection of a dovetail: when you pull on a pin board, the joint holds together even without being glued. Through dovetails are used for all sorts of boxes but especially when the builder wants to show off the construction.

Dovetail jigs: Commercial dovetail jigs come in three classes. Half-blind jigs cut only half-blind joints, through jigs cut only through joints, and combination jigs cut both types as well as a varying number of other joints, such as sliding dovetail and rounded finger joints. Most jig manufacturers offer accessory templates for cutting box joints or small dovetails.

While the designs vary quite a bit, all dovetail jigs use a similar system. The work is clamped into the jig and the router, fitted with a dovetail bit, makes the cuts following a finger template. Some templates work with a template

A half-blind dovetail jig sets up to cut the pins and the tails at the same time.

guide, while others are made for a bearing-piloted dovetail or flush-trimming bit. Often the bit and template guide are included with the jig, or the manufacturer specifies the right type to use. With half-blind jigs, the pins and tails are cut at the same time. Pins and tails for through joints are made separately. The procedure for setting up a dovetail jig is specific to the model.

Consider these features when shopping for a commerical jig:

• Construction: For any type of jig, a solid, rigid template is best. Many are heavy aluminum or phenolic resin. Plastic templates can have flexing problems, and router bases may not glide smoothly over them. Board clamps should hold the work firmly. Big knobs or handles for tightening clamps are a plus.

• Adjustable templates: Some jigs have cutting templates with adjustable fingers, allowing you to vary the spacing between pins and tails. Standard (non-adjustable) templates may be reversible for different dovetail sizes.

• Ease of use: All dovetail jigs require careful setups, but some are simpler to learn and use than others. The tradeoff is that a more complex jig may offer greater versatility.

• Capacity: The maximum size of stock that jigs can accommodate ranges between 12" and 36" wide and up to 1½" thick.

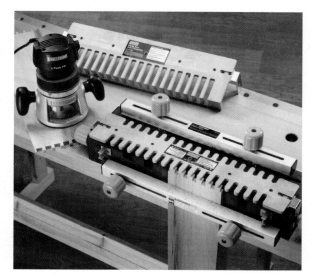

Cutting through dovetails requires separate cuts.

SLIDING DOVETAILS

A sliding dovetail essentially is a tongue-and-groove joint in which both the groove and tongue are dovetail shaped, creating a strong, interlocking connection without the need for fasteners or glue. Use them for adjustable shelves, custom box lids, casework, or table leg-to-post connections. You can make the cuts with a hand-held router, using an edge guide, a right-angle jig, or a T-square. Because the joints can be long, it's a good idea to cut first with a straight bit that matches or is slightly smaller than the neck (narrowest part) of the dovetail bit, then make a final pass with the dovetail bit.

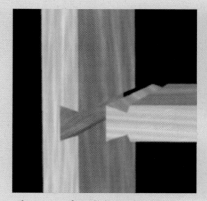

Closeup of a sliding dovetail joint.

Cut the groove for a sliding dovetail, using a right-angle jig.

Clamp 1½" blocks at both sides of workpiece and use an edge guide to cut the tail for a sliding dovetail.

Box joints. If you don't have a commercial dovetail jig that cuts box joints, you can make them on the router table using a shop-made jig. Plan your joints before building the jig. All it takes is some simple math and adherence to these criteria:

1. Box joints have equally sized fingers and notches.

2. The width of the notches and fingers is the same as the diameter of the bit used to cut them.

3. All of the notches and fingers should be full size (no half-fingers)—this means that the width of the stock must be divisible by the bit diameter.

A box joint jig makes it easy to cut perfect box joints. Use the fence or the miter slot to guide the jig.

4. The finger length is determined by the bit height and must match the thickness of the stock.

For example, if you're using a ½"-diameter bit, the stock width can be 1", 1½", 2", 2½", and so on. The notch and finger width will measure ½". If the stock is ¾" thick, set the bit height on the router table at ¾".

Build the box joint jig with ¾" plywood. Glue the fence to the base at 90°, and attach a block behind to support the fence. The fence must be a little over twice as long as the width of stock you'll be cutting. If you have a miter slot on your table, cut a guide piece to fit into the slot and attach it to the bottom of the jig, at right angles to the jig fence. Load the straight bit you'll use for the box joint cuts, and set the depth to equal the stock thickness. Guiding the jig along the router table fence or the miter slot, cut a shallow slot into the center of the jig fence. Make a hardwood or plywood stop block so its width is exactly equal to the bit diameter. Glue the block to the fence, leaving a gap between the block and the slot equal to the bit diameter.

Cut the first notch with the workpiece edge against the stop block. Fit the notch over the stop block to align the cut for the second notch.

Leave the first workpiece in place after making the last cut. Position the second workpiece against the first to make its first cut.

Use a stop block as a fulcrum for greater control when initiating a slot cut.

Test the jig for accuracy with practice cuts. Clamp the finger board on its end with one edge butted against the stop block. Make the cut by pushing the jig and board into the bit, then backing it out. Slip each new notch over the stop block to cut the remaining fingers. To set up the first cut on the notch board, leave the finger board clamped in place with its last notch over the stop block. Butt the notch board against the finger board and clamp it in place. Cut the first notch, then use the stop block to cut the remaining notches. If the joint doesn't fit well, re-adjust the table fence.

Biscuit Joints

Biscuit joints offer a simple alternative to traditional joinery and can be used in place of tongue-and-groove, mortise-and-tenon, and spline joints. A biscuit joint consists of identical curved slots cut into two mating pieces and filled with a football-shaped wood biscuit. When glued, the biscuit swells with moisture to create a tight joint. Typically biscuit slots are cut with a dedicated power tool called a biscuit, or plate, joiner, but you can make them with a router and slot cutter bit. In a router table or hand-held router, a 1⅞"-diameter, ⁵⁄₃₂" bearing-guided slot cutter (either two- or three-wing) will cut any size of standard biscuit.

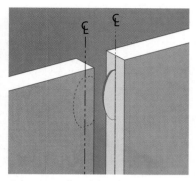

Edge-to-edge biscuit joint

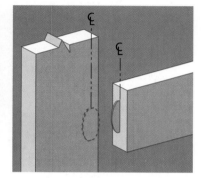

Rail-to-stile biscuit joint

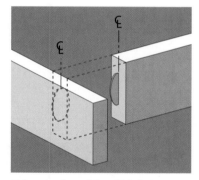

Edge-to-face biscuit joint

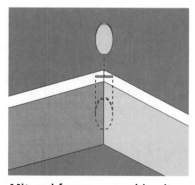

Mitered frame corner biscuit joint

FLUSH BISCUIT JOINTS

To ensure flush joints even when a biscuit slot isn't perfectly centered, mark the faces of all workpieces, then rout all the slots with the same faces positioned up.

Cutting biscuit slots on a router table: Set up the table with a $\frac{5}{32}$" slot cutter and a fence that surrounds the bit as much as possible. Mark reference lines onto the fence—centered over the bit—to locate the start and stop positions of the cut. To calculate the reference lines, subtract the diameter of the cutter from the desired slot length. For example, a standard #20 biscuit requires a $2\frac{1}{2}$"-long slot. If the slot cutter is $1\frac{7}{8}$" in diameter, the reference lines should be $\frac{5}{8}$" apart ($2\frac{1}{2}$" − $1\frac{7}{8}$" = $\frac{5}{8}$").

Next, mark the center of each slot on the workpieces (when the joints are assembled, the centerlines are matched). Set the bit height so the slot will be centered within the workpiece (see Flush Biscuit Joints, page 109). For a full-depth cut, adjust the fence so it's flush with the slot cutter's bearing; for shallower cuts, position the fence in front of the bearing.

When cutting biscuit slots on a router table, mark reference lines on the fence and workpiece to guide the cut.

To make the cut, hold the back end of the workpiece against the fence, then carefully pivot the stock into the spinning cutter, aligning the centerline of the biscuit slot with the right reference mark. When the stock is flush against the fence, feed the work to the left until the centerline meets the left reference mark, then carefully pull the work away from the cutter. Use a push sled for greater control when slotting small stock or making end cuts.

Cutting biscuit slots with a hand-held router: A hand-held router and saddle jig work well for biscuit slots made in the narrow edges of workpieces, because the stock face supports the router and jig. Slotting stock faces requires a setup that provides adequate support, but the operation is the same.

First build the jig. To determine the gap between the jig fences, add the diameter of your router's subbase to the reference mark offset described in the router table

To create a slotting saddle jig, determine the spacing needed between the fences. The jig needs to be wide enough to allow for the router bit to extend between the jig and the face of the workpiece.

Make the slot cut by starting at the left and moving to the right.

procedure above. For example, if the slot size is 2½", the cutter is 1⅞", and the subbase is 6", set the fences 6⅝" apart (2½" − 1⅞" = ⅝"; 6" + ⅝" = 6⅝"). Mark the slot centerlines onto the workpiece faces, and set the bit depth so the slot is centered along the stock edge (see Flush Biscuit Joints, page 109). Clamp the jig to the work so the fences are centered over the slot mark and perpendicular to the edges. Make the cut by plunging into the stock while guiding the subbase along the left fence. When the cutter bearing contacts the stock edge, feed the router to the right until it contacts the right fence, then carefully back out the cutter.

Rail & Stile Joints

Rail-and-stile joinery, also called cope-and-stick, is a form of decorative frame construction used for making frame-and-panel cabinet doors and traditional wall paneling. Specialty router bits allow you to cut the frame joints along with the profiled edges and continuous groove that receives the panel. Panels can be flat, or you can use a special bit to mill the edges of thicker panels for a classic raised panel assembly.

Rail-and-stile bits: These are available in three styles. Matched bit sets include two bits—one stile cutter and one rail cutter. They are the easiest type to use and generally require the shortest setup time, so they're usually worth the extra cost. A reversible rail-and-stile bit can make both cuts, but you must disassemble and reverse the cutters to do so, and setting up the cuts can be trying. A third type is the stacked bit, which has the rail and stile cutters stacked on the same arbor. Instead of reversing the cutters, you raise and lower the stacked bit to make the two cuts. All rail-and-stile bits come in a range of decorative profiles, and all should be used only on the router table.

Panel cabinet doors made with rail-and-stile joinery are common in fine cabinetry and can be created with three bits (inset). Standard rail-and-stile frames are ¾" thick, but most bits can cut ⅝" to ⅞" stock.

Make the stile cuts, using featherboards to stabilize the long, thin stock.

To set the height of the rail bit, use one of the stile test pieces as a gauge. Align the tongue-cutting portion of the bit with the stile's groove.

Use scrap pieces of stock to create a test joint to get the proper fit.

Cut a rail end edge along a scrap piece to form a backer for cutting the rail ends. Fit the stile cutout into the scrap, and feed the rail into the bit, outer side first.

Cutting rail-and-stile joints: When preparing the stock for your project, make extra pieces to use for test cuts and for a backer piece used when milling the rail ends. To simplify assembly, you can cut all of the pieces a little long—trim the rails to length after making the stile cuts, and trim the stiles flush to the rails after the glued frame has dried. Be aware that the longest point on the rail piece is the tongue. To get the proper dimensions, add the length of the two tongues to the desired rail length. Because the tongues are typically ⅜", this will add ¾" to the length of the rail. Some woodworkers like to make their door frames using stock about ⅛" wider than the final dimensions, so they can trim the doors to fit after they're assembled.

Start by making test cuts using scrap pieces cut from the good stock. Note: All four pieces of a frame have their inside edges milled with the stile cutter, while only the ends of the rails are cut with the rail cutter. Load the stile bit and set the height to cut the desired reveal (typically 3/32" to ⅛"). Using a thin straightedge, adjust the fence so it's flush with the bit's bearing. Rout two test pieces face-down, using hold-downs and a sled or push stick as needed for safe operation.

When using a horizontal bit, set the fence flush to the bit bearing. Use hold-downs and a push sled as needed for a safe cut. Adjust the bit height to make the cuts incrementally.

Change to the rail bit. Using one of the stile test pieces as a gauge, set the bit height so the tongue-cutting portion of the bit is aligned with the stile's groove. Position the fence so it's flush with the bit bearing, then rout an end of one of the test pieces using a push sled to stabilize the work. The bit's configuration determines whether the stock should be face-up or face-down. Check the fit of the joint. If it shows gaps or isn't flush, adjust the fence and make more test cuts.

Once the fit is acceptable, make a backer piece using the rail bit to mill the long edge of a scrap piece. Use

Cut panels with a vertical panel bit using a tall fence for support. A raised featherboard helps keep the panel tight to the fence. Control the depth of cut with the fence adjustment.

the backer to prevent tearout when cutting the ends of the rails. Also keep the final test pieces for setting up the bits for the real cuts. Cut the finish frame pieces following the same sequence used for the test cuts. Make the stile cuts on all of the frame pieces, then make the end cuts on the rails, using the rail bit.

Making raised panels: Raised panels are made with a single router bit on the router table. The bit cuts a profiled reveal into the face of the panel and creates a flat tongue along the perimeter that matches the groove in the rail-and-stile frame. Because there's no accurate method for indexing panel cuts, it's best to cut gradually and test the panel in the frame grooves until you achieve a good fit.

If you're building frame-and-panel doors, decide whether the front panel face will be flush to the front of the frame, project beyond the frame, or be recessed. The back of the panel can be flush, which requires cuts on the back side, or be left flat to create an inset from the back of the frame. Most cabinet doors with ¾"-thick frames have ⅝"- or ¾"-thick panels. You can use a solid panel (usually only if the doors are narrow) or panels made from glued-up boards. It's critical that the panels are flat and have uniform thickness.

Raised panel bits: There are two main types of raised panel bits, both of which are available in a variety of decorative profiles. Horizontal raised panel bits are large, flat cutters, commonly 3½" in diameter, that cut with the panel face-down on the table. The sheer size of these bits creates some challenges. They typically require a 2½ hp router with variable speed and should be run at about 10,000 rpm. Also, the router's base and the bit hole in the table have to accommodate the bit's diameter.

Dry-fit the rails and stiles and measure the diagonals to make sure it is square. Measure the inside dimensions of the frame to determine the panel size.

The back of the panel will be recessed from the frame unless the panel is rabbeted to make it flush.

Dry-fit the panel in the frame.

Vertical raised panel bits are tall and have less than half the diameter of horizontal bits. You can run them in a 1½ hp router, often at the standard tool speed. They are generally considered safer to use than horizontal panel bits. However, because the panels are cut on-edge, vertical bits can be difficult to use with large panels. With any type of raised panel bit, it is critical for safety and cut quality to make the cuts incrementally, removing at most ⅛" of material with each pass.

Cutting raised panels: Determine the size of each panel by measuring the frame it will fill. To calculate the width, measure between the inside edges of the stiles, then add twice the groove depth from each side. Subtract ³⁄₁₆" to ¼" from the width to allow for expansion. (If the panel is wider than 12", subtract an additional ⅛" for each additional 12" of panel width.) To calculate the panel's length, measure between the inside edges of the rails, add twice the groove depth, then subtract ¹⁄₁₆" from the total to provide some wiggle room during assembly. Cut the panels to size.

Set up the router table with a raised panel bit. If you're using a vertical bit, adjust the bit height to equal the desired amount of reveal, then set the fence to expose about ⅛" of the cutter. With a horizontal bit, set the fence flush with the bearing, and adjust the bit height for a ⅛" cut. Rout the panel with the front face against the fence (or face-down on the table), cutting the end-grain edges first, then the long-grain edges. If you're using ¾"-thick stock and want it to be flush at the back, rout the back-side edges after completing the front.

Visually test the fit against a frame piece to make sure the setup is accurate, then move the fence or raise the bit and make another pass. Repeat the process until the tongue of the panel fits easily but snugly into the frame grooves. If you're making back-side cuts, stop routing the back side when the back face is flush with the frame.

Project: Frame & Panel Door

A well-built frame-and-panel door is as attractive as it is strong. Following traditional design, this door is made with mortise-and-tenon joints—the strongest frame joint—with haunched tenons to add extra protection against twisting in the frame. The frame is made from ¾" hardwood stock and the panel is ¼" plywood with a hardwood veneer that matches the frame wood. You can substitute glass for the wood panel or use a veneer that contrasts with the frame material. The muntins dividing the top portion of the door add a Craftsman-style detail; this optional embellishment is decorative and not part of the door's structure.

MATERIALS

Note: Cut all pieces to fit
- ¾ × 2¼" hardwood for stiles and rails
- ¼" plywood panel
- ¼ × ¾" hardwood muntin stock

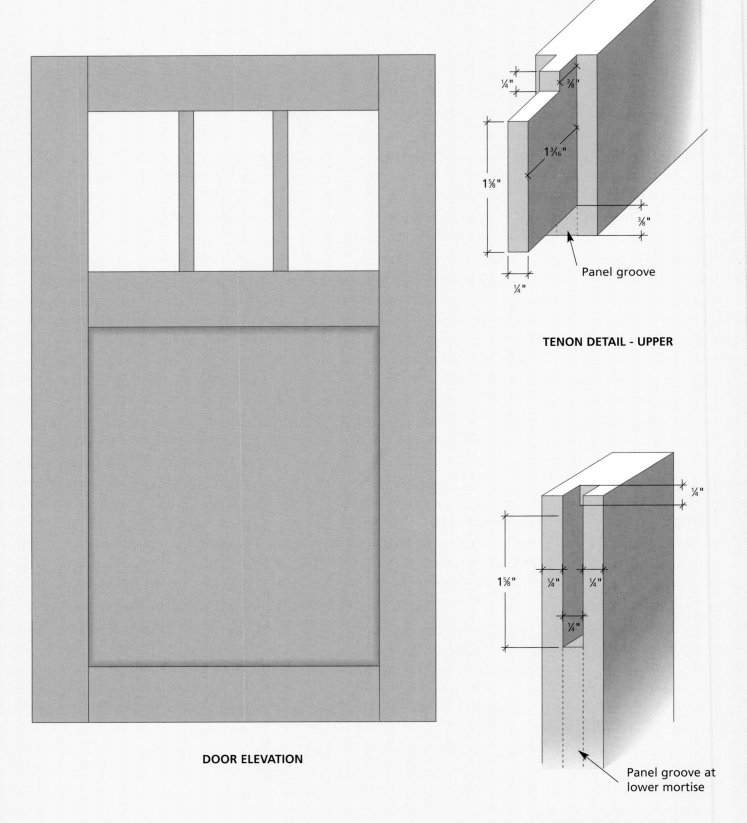

DOOR ELEVATION

TENON DETAIL - UPPER

Panel groove

1⁷⁄₁₆ "

1⅝ "

¼ "

⅜ "

¼ "

MORTISE DETAIL - UPPER

Panel groove at lower mortise

1⅝ "

¼ "

¼ "

¼ "

¼ "

How to Build the Frame & Panel Door

Step 1. Cut the stiles and rails to length. Be sure to account for the 1¾₆"-long tenons at the ends of the rails. Lay out ¼"-wide × 1⅝"-long mortises centered on the inside edges of the stiles. The outside ends of mortises should be ¼" from the ends of the stiles. Rout the mortises 1¼" deep, using one of the methods shown on pages 100 and 101.

Step 2. Cut the tenons to fit the mortises, using the table router technique shown on page 101. Cut the short inner shoulders at ⅜". On the top and bottom rails, do not make shoulder cuts on the outer ends of the tenons. Notch the outside corner of each tenon to create the ¼"-tall × ⅜"-long haunch, using a handsaw or band saw. On the middle rail make standard tenons.

Step 3. Mill ¼"-wide × ⅜"-deep grooves for the panel using a ¼" straight or spiral bit on the router table. The rail grooves are through grooves, centered along the inside edges. The stile grooves are stopped grooves. Stop the stile grooves at the mortise for the middle rail. At the top of the stiles, rout a groove from the end to the mortise to accommodate the top rail haunch. Test-fit the groove over the panel stock.

Step 4. Round over the bottom ends of the tenons to fit the mortises. Dry-assemble the frame, clamp it, and make sure it's square. Measure the inside dimensions of the frame to determine the panel size. Cut the panel ⅝" longer and wider than the inner frame dimensions. Glue the frame joints and assemble the door with the panel fitted into the frame grooves. Do not glue the panel in place. Clamp the assembly and check it for square before letting it dry. If desired, cut the muntins to fit between the frame members and glue them to the panel and the frame edges.

Rout the mortises in the rails, using edge-guide technique.

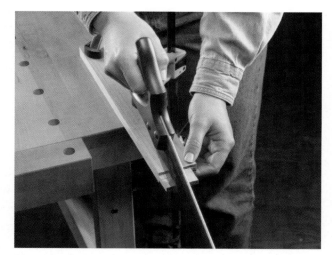
Use a backsaw to cut the haunches ¼" × ⅜" long for the tenons.

Cut the panel grooves on the router table.

Cut the muntins to fit and glue them in place.

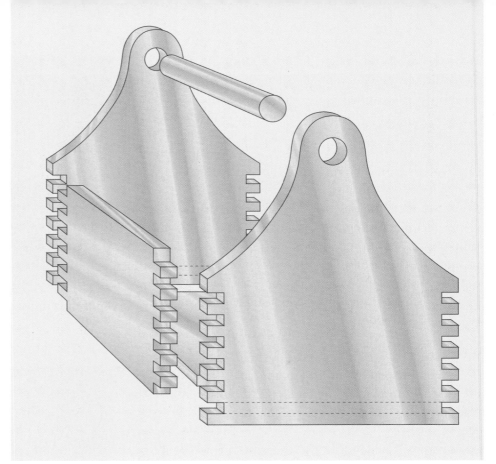

Carpenter's Toolbox

With its box-jointed sides and shaped ends, this easy-to-build toolbox will show off your routing skills for years to come. The box is strong enough to carry a full load of tools and works equally well as an indoor piece. All the dimensions are given to build the project as shown. You can change the sizes of any of the pieces or the fingers of the box joints; just make sure the width of the sides is divisible by the diameter of the bit you use to cut the joints. If you plan to use the box outdoors, glue the joints with waterproof glue.

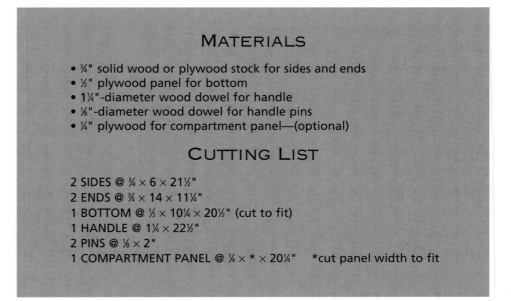

MATERIALS

- ¾" solid wood or plywood stock for sides and ends
- ½" plywood panel for bottom
- 1¼"-diameter wood dowel for handle
- ⅛"-diameter wood dowel for handle pins
- ¼" plywood for compartment panel—(optional)

CUTTING LIST

2 SIDES @ ¾ × 6 × 21½"
2 ENDS @ ¾ × 14 × 11¼"
1 BOTTOM @ ½ × 10¼ × 20½" (cut to fit)
1 HANDLE @ 1¼ × 22½"
2 PINS @ ⅛ × 2"
1 COMPARTMENT PANEL @ ¼ × * × 20¼"   *cut panel width to fit

END VIEW

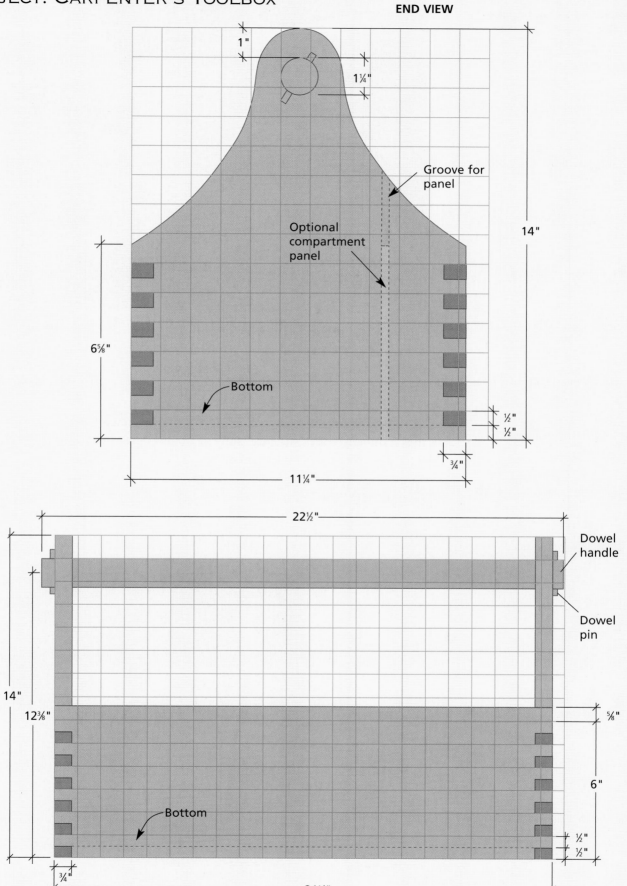

1"

1¼"

Groove for panel

Optional compartment panel

14"

6⅝"

Bottom

½"
½"

¾"

11¼"

22½"

Dowel handle

Dowel pin

14"

12⅜"

⅝"

6"

Bottom

½"
½"

¾"

21½"

SIDE VIEW

Cut the box joints on the end blanks before routing it to shape.

How to Build the Carpenter's Toolbox

Step 1. Cut the sides and end blanks to size. Make box joint cuts on the ends of all four pieces, using a commercial template or the box joint jig shown on page 108. The fingers and notches are ½" wide × ¾" deep.

Step 2. Dry-assemble the box to make sure the joints fit properly. Measure the inside dimensions of the box, and cut the bottom to size so it is ⁷⁄₁₆" wider and longer than the inner box dimensions. Disassemble the box. Mill a ½"-wide × ¼"-deep groove into each piece, locating the bottom of the groove ½" from the bottom edge. The end piece gets through grooves; make sure the grooves are perfectly aligned with the lowest box joint notches. On the side pieces, stop the grooves ½" from the ends of the sides. Mill the grooves using a ½" straight or

Stop the grooves on the side pieces to preserve the finger joints. Check the fit.

spiral bit and a plunge router with an edge guide or on the router table. Test-fit the bottom in the grooves. Square the ends of the stopped grooves with a chisel.

If you're adding a compartment panel, cut ¼"-wide × ⅛"-deep vertical grooves on the inside faces of the end piece. You can locate the panel anywhere you like, but make sure the grooves are aligned with each other.

Step 3. Shape the end pieces following the diagram on page 119. Cut the profile using a jig saw or coping saw, or make a template and cut the shapes with a router. Cut the holes for the handle to match the dowel diameter.

Rout the ends to shape using a template and a flush-trimming bit.

Step 4. Glue the joint fingers and assemble the toolbox. Do not glue the bottom piece in the grooves. Clamp the assembly and let it dry. Cut the dowel to length and feed it though the holes in the ends so it overhangs evenly on both sides. Mark and drill pin holes through the center of the dowel, then glue the pins in the holes.

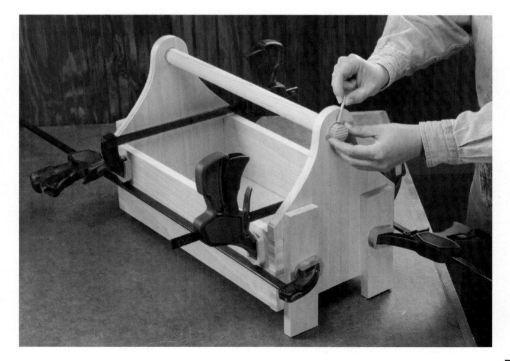

Insert the dowel pins and glue them in place.

Chapter 7
TEMPLATE ROUTING

Template routing exploits the router's unique ability to make patterned cuts. The procedure is perfectly simple: affix a template to the workpiece, then rout around the edges of the template to create an exact copy. Virtually any shape is possible, and the router will duplicate the template accurately every time. In addition to cutting shapes, you can use templates to make precise cutouts, excavations, holes, and slots, and to create inlays. Custom work with shop-made templates greatly expands the creative possibilities of routing. On the more practical side, commercial templates help take the guesswork (and fear) out of construction cuts that leave no room for error, such as hinge-mortising and countertop installations.

Template Basics

There are two main types of setups in template routing. The difference lies in the bits used. If you make the cuts with a bearing-guided pattern bit or flush-trimming bit, the bearing travels along the template edge and the bit trims the workpiece flush, creating an exact duplicate. The alternative setup involves a non-piloted bit used with a template guide (see Template Guides, page 125). In this configuration, the guide follows the template while the exposed portion of the bit below makes the cut. The finished workpiece has the same shape as the template, but is a slightly different size, due to the offset between the outside of the template guide and the cutting edge of the bit. You compensate for the offset by making the template slightly smaller or larger than the finished workpiece. The following chart summarizes the pros and cons of the different configurations.

TEMPLATE ROUTING SETUPS

SETUP	ADVANTAGES	DISADVANTAGES
Pattern bit (bearing at top of bit)	Template is same size as workpiece Plunge cuts possible Multiple cuts possible on thick stock	Full bit extension required with thin template
Flush-trimming bit (bearing at bottom of bit)	Template is same size as workpiece Easy setup on router table, reduced bit exposure	All cuts are full depth
Template guide	Greatest bit selection Can use multiple bits with same guide Plunge and shallow cuts possible, with guide always contacting template	Template size must account for offset No exact duplication of objects (see Using Objects for Templates, page 127)

Making Your Own Templates

Templates are easiest to make using thin, ¼" to ½" sheet materials, including plywood, hardboard, MDF, and plastic. The best material thickness to use depends on the application. The thin edges of ¼" hardboard are easy to cut and smooth, but the template won't withstand long-term use as well as ½" plywood or MDF. Voids in plywood edges can be a problem, so use cabinet-grade material if possible. Also consider the bit setup to make sure the template isn't too thick to permit a full cut or too thin for your template guide. If you're using a pattern bit, a thick template will give you some control over the depth of cut.

A flush-trimming bit with a bottom bearing rides along a template placed below the workpiece.

TEMPLATE GUIDES

Template guides, also called collar guides, are metal fittings that attach to the router's subbase and have a cylindrical collar that surrounds the bit. The collar rides along a template to control the cut, eliminating the need for a pilot bearing. There are guides made for specific router brands, as well as universal systems that are compatible with several different router makes. Ask the manufacturer about which systems will work for your router. Guides may attach with a locknut, screws, or a twist-lock fitting.

Template guides come in a range of sizes, with three important dimensions: the inner and outer diameters of the collar and the distance the collar projects from the subbase. The collar's inner diameter must be larger than the overall diameter of the bit (dovetail bits are an exception, because their cutters remain below the collar). For template work, the smaller the outer diameter of the guide, the better it will be at following fine detail and making sharp turns. The collar projection, which ranges from about $\frac{5}{32}$" to over $\frac{1}{2}$", is important because the template must be thicker than the projection. However, you can grind down or hacksaw a little off the collar projection without affecting the guide's performance.

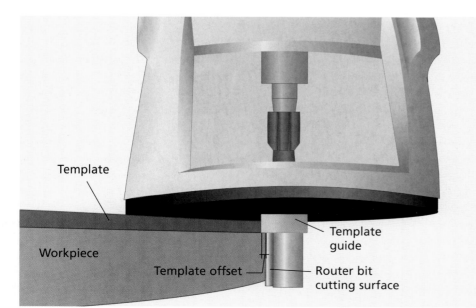

A template guide eliminates the need for a pilot bearing on the bit. Using a template guide does result in an offset between the size of the template and the final size of the workpiece.

Template

Workpiece

Template offset

Template guide

Router bit cutting surface

Cutting around the outside edge of a template with a flush-cutting bit results in an exact match (left). Cutting around the inside of a cutout template results in rounded corners due to the radius of the bit or the template guide collar (right).

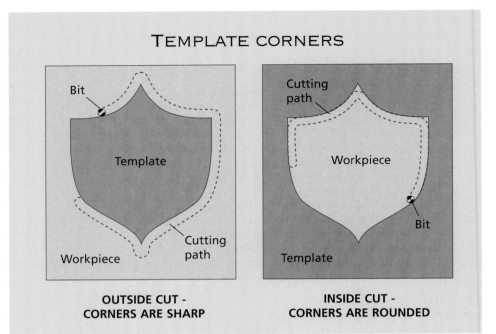

TEMPLATE CORNERS

Bit

Template

Workpiece

Cutting path

OUTSIDE CUT - CORNERS ARE SHARP

Cutting path

Workpiece

Bit

Template

INSIDE CUT - CORNERS ARE ROUNDED

How you make the template also depends on the bit setup. Working with a template guide requires an extra step when laying out the template, but otherwise the procedure is the same. Keep in mind that the quality of the template translates directly to the quality of the finished workpiece, so make the template with care. Start by drawing a full-size outline of the pattern onto your template stock. The sharpness of the corners is determined by whether the cut is around the outside of the template or within a cutout in the template (see above illustration). If you're using a template guide, re-trace the pattern outline, adding or subtracting the offset of the guide. Make the outline smaller for

To allow for the offset of the template guide, add or subtract the offset dimension from your template size.

Template edges must be perfectly smooth. Any irregularities will transfer to the finished piece. Use a file or sanding block to smooth or straighten corners.

outside cuts, larger for inside cuts. Cut the template along the outline using a jig saw, band saw, scroll saw, or coping saw. Smooth all the lines with a file and sandpaper. Any bumps or dips left on the template will show up on your workpiece.

Using Objects for Templates

An alternative to making templates from scratch is to use an object itself as a template or to make a template using an object as the pattern. With a pattern or flush-trimming bit, you can secure an object, such as an old plaque or table-

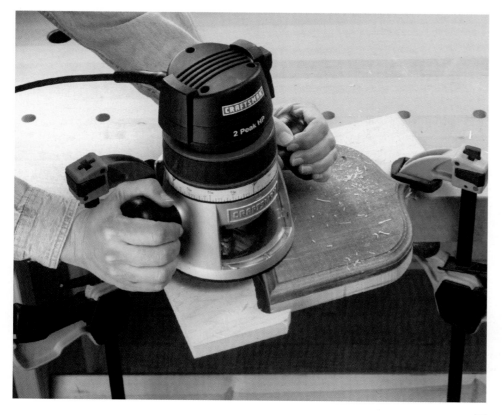

By using a pattern or flush-trimming bit, you can create duplicates of many objects without making a separate pattern.

To duplicate a straight-sided item without measuring, simply secure scrap pieces around the object.

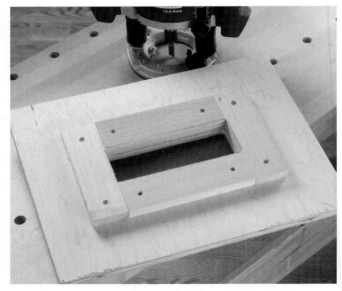

Use a plunge router with a flush-trimming bit to cut out the window template.

top, directly to the workpiece, then trim around it to create a duplicate. To make a template using an object, place the item over your template stock and surround it with pieces of scrap material fixed to the template. Cut out the area defined by the scrap pieces to create a "window" template.

Template Routing Techniques

Template cuts can be made with a hand-held router or on the router table. Minimize wear on your router by tracing the template outline onto the workpiece and trimming most of the waste with a saw before routing. For a template guide setup, trace around the template with a compass to add the offset. Saw the workpiece to within $\frac{1}{16}$" to $\frac{1}{8}$" of the outline. Clamp the template and work securely. If conventional clamps will get in the way, use hot glue or double-

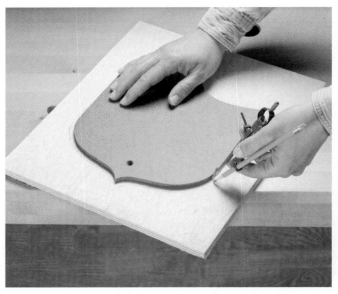

To remove excess stock before routing, use a compass to mark slightly outside the final dimensions of the workpiece.

Use a band saw or jig saw to cut along the rough outline, then attach the template and rout the final cut.

sided tape to stick the template to the workpiece and the workpiece to your bench. Use the same methods for the router table, or build a jig to hold the work as you move it over the bit.

With a hand-held router, make the template cut using a conventional feed: feed the router counterclockwise for outside template cuts; clockwise for inside cuts. A plunge router fitted with a pattern bit or template guide allows you to plunge into interior cuts and make partial-depth interior groove cuts. For stock that is thicker than bit capacity, use a pattern bit and make two passes. On the second pass, the bearing follows the cut made in the first pass. You can also make the second pass with a flush-trimming bit, cutting from the other face of the stock.

Template cuts on the router table involve the same techniques used for edge-forming (see Routing without a fence, page 73). You can use a pattern or flush-trimming bit or a template guide setup. For a pattern bit or template guide, stick the template to the bottom of the workpiece. A flush-trimming bit works with the template on top of the stock, making it easier to watch the bearing as it follows the template. Always use a bit guard and a starting pin or fulcrum to stabilize the workpiece.

When cutting thick material using a template and a flush-trimming bit, adjust the bit depth so the bearing runs along the template for the first cut. For successive cutting depths, the bearing will run along the previously cut stock.

DRILLING HOLES

With the aid of a template and template guide, your plunge router can drill holes as cleanly as a drill press. Cut holes in the template to match the diameter of the template guide's collar. Use a plunge-cutting straight or spiral bit to cut the holes in the workpiece.

Curved Edge-joining

Joining workpieces with matching irregular edges is one of the best tricks of template routing. The process requires three templates. The first is the original template, which you outline, cut, and smooth as with a standard template. Then, using the original pattern as a template, you rout a left and a right cutting template; these are used to make the final workpiece cuts.

The key to matching curved cuts is to compensate for the material removed by the bit. You accomplish this by using a bit and template guide (or over-sized pilot bearing) that have an offset equal to ½ of the bit diameter. In the example shown here, a ⅜" bit is used with a ¾" (outer diameter) template guide. The offset is 3/16". You can use a bit and guide of different sizes, as long as the offset is ½ of the bit diameter.

Curved edge-joining involves making three templates. Use the first template to cut the left and right templates.

Start by drawing the curved pattern onto the original template. Keep in mind that the final joint shape will be slightly different from this original pattern, due to the offset. Cut the template along the line, then smooth the edge with a file and sandpaper. Clamp the original template over a single board of stock you're using for the left and right cutting templates, aligning the side edges. Using the ⅜" bit and ¾" template guide, cut completely through the stock board to create the two new templates. Note: You can also make this cut with a ⅜" pattern or flush-trimming bit. Mark the left and right templates. Because of the material removed, these two templates will not fit together perfectly.

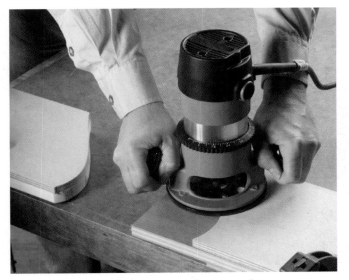

Cut each piece with the appropriate template.

After cutting, test-fit the pieces together to make sure they fit securely.

Make the cuts in the workpieces using the left and right templates. Align the side edge of each template and workpiece to reference the cuts. Rout the workpieces using the ⅜" bit and ¾" template guide.

Inlays

Inlay work adds a distinctive touch of craftsmanship to any piece. Most often used as decoration, inlays can also hide knots and other stock defects. Installing an inlay is a basic template-routing operation. It's a job for a hand-held router (preferably a plunge router) and an inlay kit—a set with a template guide, a bushing that fits over the guide's collar, and a bit, typically a ⅛" down-spiral bit. The bushing creates on offset equal to the bit diameter. Inlay kits are commonly available through bit manufacturers.

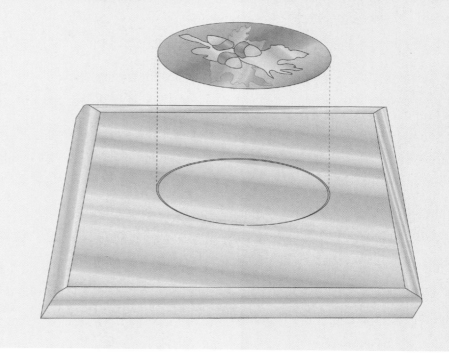

Inlay kits make it possible to create fine decorative panels, like the one shown here.

The inlay process involves cutting a recess using a shop-made template and the inlay kit with the bushing in place. Then, you cut the inlay insert, this time without the bushing, using the same template used to make the recess. Glue the insert into the recess and sand it flush to complete the detail.

Start by making the template. Use a material that's just slightly thicker than the inlay kit's bushing; a thick template would require greater extension of the fragile ⅛" bit, increasing the chance of breakage. The overall size of the template

Once you have determined the size and shape of the inlay, size the template to allow for the template guide offset.

must provide adequate support for the router base. Draw the outline of the inlay onto the template stock, then enlarge the outline by a margin equal to the offset (⅛" in this example). The inner outline is the actual size of the inlay. Make sure any inside corners or curves on the outer pattern have a radius that's no smaller than the radius of the bushing. Cut the template to the outer pattern line, and file and sand the edges smooth.

Rout the recess next. Secure the template to the workpiece with clamps or double-sided tape. Set up your router with the template guide, bushing, and inlay bit. Set the bit depth to cut just shy of the thickness of the insert stock. If the inlay is small, you can rout the entire recess with the inlay bit: work outward from the center to clear away the material. For larger

For large inlays, rout the outline with the inlay bit, then remove the remaining waste with a large straight bit.

inlays, rout along the perimeter of the template cutout with the inlay bit to establish the outline of the recess, then switch to a larger straight bit to clean out the rest of the recess. In either case, rout along the template edges twice to make sure the recess is complete.

Cut the insert using the inlay bit and template guide without the bushing. Lay the insert stock over a scrap board to protect your workbench. To keep the insert from coming free and possibly getting damaged as the bit finishes the cut, place a strip of double-sided tape between the insert stock and the scrap backer. Clamp or tape the template over the insert stock. Set the bit depth to cut com-

Secure the inlay to scrap wood with tape. Use the inlay bit and template guide without the bushing to cut the inlay to size.

Apply glue to the bottom of the recess and the back of the inlay piece, and join the pieces.

pletely through the stock. Make the cut by carefully following the edges of the template cutout. Any deviation from the edge will misshape the insert. Check the fit of the insert in the recess. Brush an even coating of glue over the recess floor and sides. Tap the insert into the recess using a mallet or a hammer and block. After the glue dries, sand the insert flush to the workpiece surface.

Commercial Templates

Commercial templates are available for a variety of jobs that require a high degree of accuracy. The most popular router templates are hinge mortisers. These range from simple plastic plates that you clamp to the door edge, to precision rack systems that help you make perfectly spaced mortises on both the door and the jamb. The size of the template opening corresponds to the leaf of the hinge; as many butt hinges have rounded corners, you cut the mortise with a bit that matches the corners' radius. Mortising, or hinge-mortising, bits have flat cutters specifically designed for efficient, smooth-bottomed mortise cuts.

Placing and cutting hinge mortises is simplified by using a hinge mortise kit. A special mortising bit (inset) cuts smooth-bottomed mortises.

The precision router work required for solid-surfacing has produced a number of commercial templates and guides that are equally useful for woodworking. Solid-aluminum straightedges are available in lengths up to 150", great for routing long runs of countertop or trimming sheet goods. Squares and radiusing templates help you make precise angle cuts in a variety of angles, or round off corners with exact curves. Less-industrial commercial templates include plastic radius guides for rounding the corners of tabletops and other surfaces, and picture frame and plaque templates.

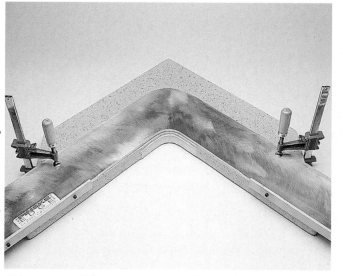

Photo courtesy of The Pinske Edge

This commercial countertop template is for radiusing solid-surface countertop corners, but it is also ideal for radiusing tabletops.

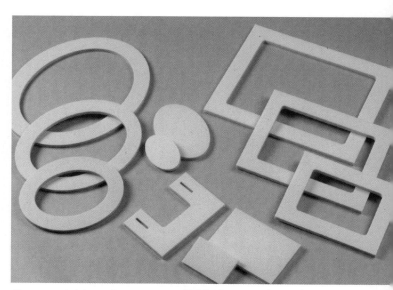

Commercial templates are available for a variety of projects, such as picture frames and cabinet hinge mortises.

Decorative shelves are easy to make with a router.

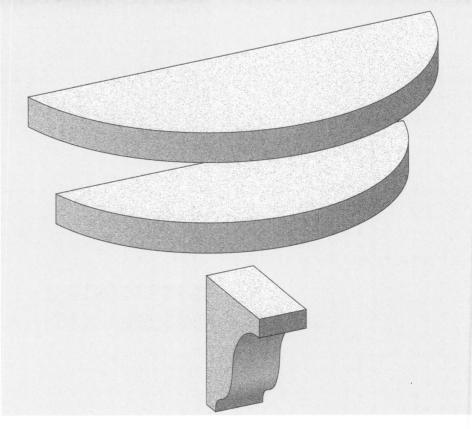

Project: Decorative Shelves

Small display shelves have strength in numbers. You can hang them in a grouping on a single wall, or use a pair for flanking a headboard, bathroom mirror, fireplace mantel, or doorway. With template routing techniques, it's easy to build identical custom shelf units like the one in this project. Two router bits—one for cutting the pieces, plus a keyhole bit to make the mounting holes—are required to complete the project as shown. The brackets can be made with 2 × 4 material (1½" thick) or two pieces of ½" MDF glued together. You may want to shape the edges of the shelf and bracket with a decorative edge-forming bit or create your own shelf design using the construction steps given here.

MATERIALS

- 10 × 12" piece of ½" MDF
- *8"-long piece of 2 × 4 *optional material for brackets
- ¼" hardboard or other template material
- Wood glue
- Finishing materials

How to Build the Decorative Shelf

Step 1. Make templates for the top and bottom shelf pieces and the bracket, using ¼" hardboard or other template stock of your choice. Use a strip of cardboard as a trammel to draw the curves for the shelf pieces. Poke a nail through the cardboard to create a pivot point. Measure from the point and make two holes for the tip of a pencil, one at 4⅞" and one at 5⅝". Draw a straight line on the template stock, about 1½" from one of the long edges, then draw a perpendicular centerline through the original line. Measure from the intersection of these lines and mark a pivot point at 1³⁄₁₆".

Decorative shelf

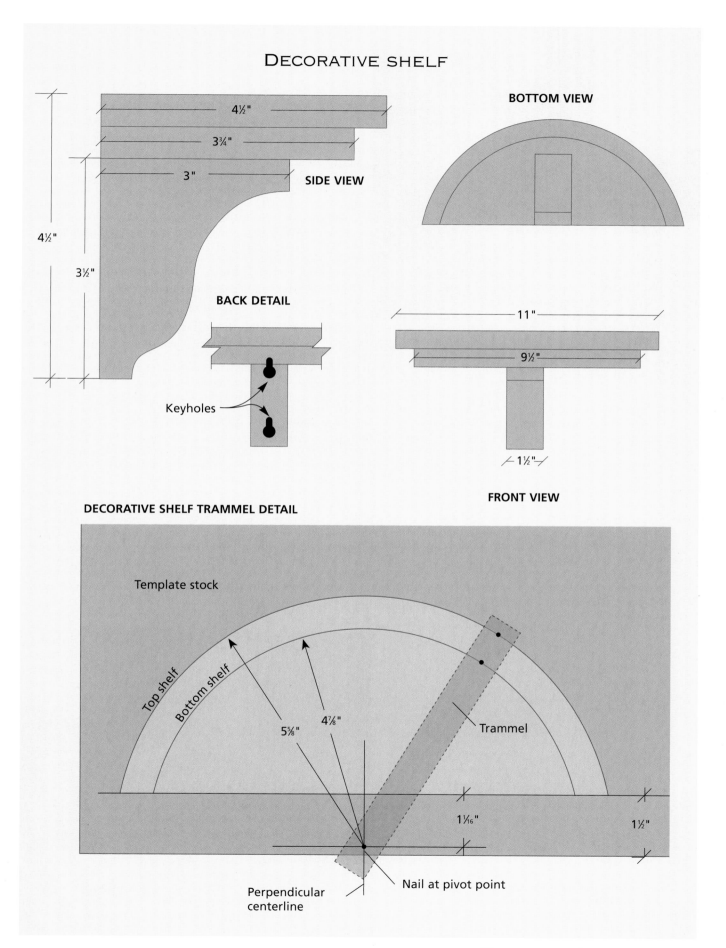

4½"

3¾"

3"

SIDE VIEW

4½"

3½"

BOTTOM VIEW

BACK DETAIL

Keyholes

11"

9½"

1½"

FRONT VIEW

DECORATIVE SHELF TRAMMEL DETAIL

Template stock

Top shelf

Bottom shelf

5⅝"

4⅞"

Trammel

1 1/16"

1½"

Nail at pivot point

Perpendicular
centerline

Position each template along a straight factory edge of the stock to minimize cutting.

Drive the nail through the trammel's pivot point and into the pivot point on the template. Use a pencil placed in the farther pencil hole to draw the curve for the top shelf piece. Repeat the process on the opposite edge of the template stock, and draw the curve for the bottom shelf piece using the nearer pencil hole. Draw the shape of the bracket onto the template stock. Cut out the three templates, then trim and smooth the edges as described in Making Your Own Templates, starting on page 124.

Step 2. Use the templates to trace the shelf outlines onto ½" MDF stock. Rough-cut the pieces with a jig saw, band saw, or coping saw. Trace and cut the bracket pieces from the leftover MDF or from 2 × 4 stock. Template-rout each piece to finished size, following the steps described in Template Routing Techniques, starting on page 128. To cut the full thickness of the 2 × 4 brackets, make two passes with a pattern bit, or cut to partial depth with a pattern bit or template guide, and make a final pass with a flush-trimming bit.

Step 3. Assemble the shelf with glue. If you're making the bracket with ½" stock, glue the two halves together first. Glue the bottom shelf piece centered under the top shelf piece, and the bracket centered under the bottom shelf piece. Make sure all pieces are flush along their back edges. Clamp the assembly and let it dry.

Step 4. Draw a centerline down the back of the shelf unit. Clamp the unit backside up, and rout a keyhole slot into the back edge of the bottom shelf and the bracket, centering both holes on the line. Orient the slots with the access holes down. Finish the shelf as desired. To hang the shelves, measure between the centers of the access holes of the keyhole slots to determine the spacing between the mounting screws.

Rout the keyhole slots on the vertical centerline.

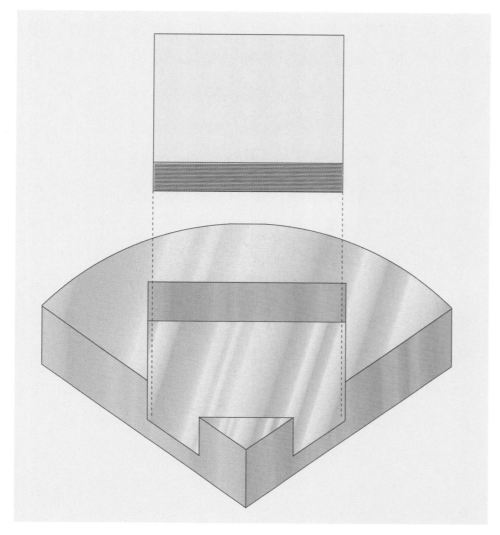

Project: Notepad Holder

This handy desktop accessory is an attractive alternative to cheap, plastic office supplies. It's designed to hold standard 3 × 3" sticky notes, but you can modify the center recess to accommodate personal stationery, business cards, etc. Made from a single 5 × 5" piece of ¾" plywood or solid lumber, the holder is a good project for practicing template routing and makes a great (and economical) gift.

MATERIALS

- 5 × 5" square of ¾" cabinet-grade plywood or solid stock—at least two adjacent sides must be straight and square
- Template stock
- Double-sided tape
- Finishing materials
- Stick-on rubber pads

PROJECT: NOTEPAD HOLDER

TEMPLATE DIAGRAM

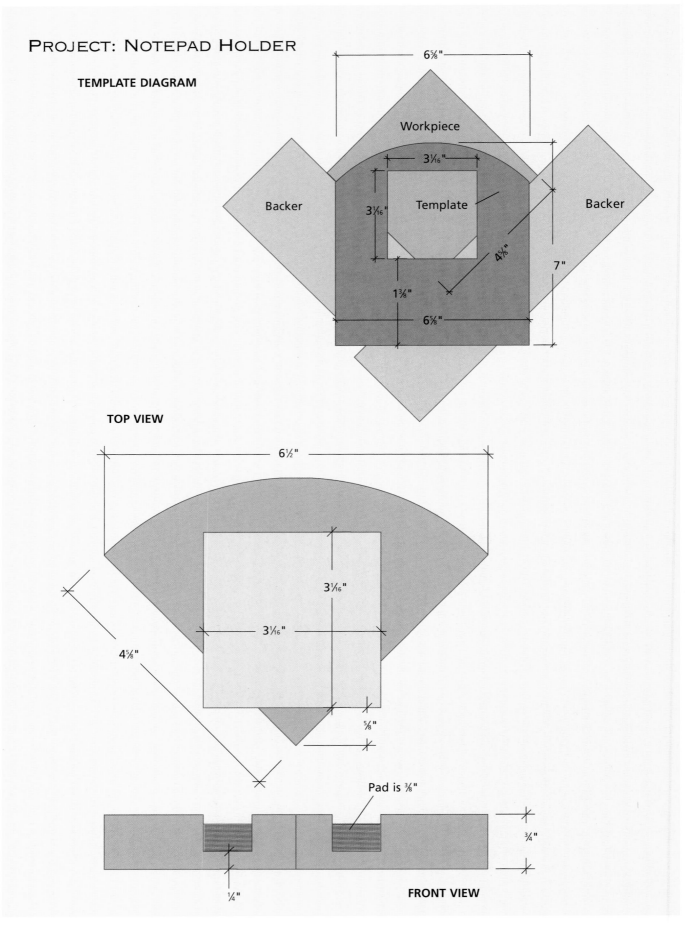

TOP VIEW

Pad is ⅜"

FRONT VIEW

How to Make the Notepad Holder

Step 1. Cut the template following the diagram on page 138, using the techniques described in Making Your Own Templates, starting on page 124. This template is designed for use with a flush-cutting pattern bit; if you plan to make the template cuts with a template guide, size the template appropriately for your setup. File and sand the edges of the template so they are perfectly smooth. Test-fit the center cutout for accuracy using a standard 3×3" sticky notepad.

Drill a starter hole, then cut out the opening in the template, using a jig saw.

Step 2. If you'd like to chamfer the outside edges of your holder, make the cuts on the two adjacent edges that will be at the front of the holder. The edges are less likely to tear out if you shape them now rather than after the template cuts are made. Place the template over the workpiece so the back corners of the template are aligned with the side edges of the workpiece. Trace the back curve onto the stock, then trim the waste to within ⅛" of the line, following the steps described in Template Routing Techniques, starting on page 128.

Secure the workpiece to a platform of scrap material (you'll be cutting into the scrap) with double-sided tape. Clamp two ¾"-thick scrap backer pieces against the front edges of the workpiece to prevent tearout. Tape the template to the workpiece. Using a plunge-cutting straight or spiral bit, rout the center recess with a series of ⅛"-deep passes until reaching a final depth of ½". If you're using a pattern bit (bearing on top), freehand the initial passes, staying away from the edges of the template. When you reach full depth and the bearing will contact the template, rout along the perimeter to complete the cutout. Rout along the back edge with a full-depth cut.

Step 3. Remove the template. Carefully square the back corners of the cutout, using a sharp chisel. Sand and finish the holder, then apply stick-on rubber pads to the corners of the bottom.

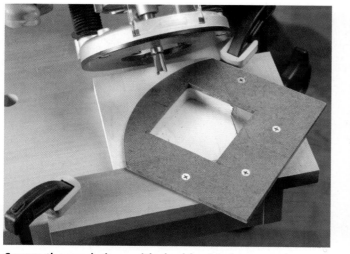

Secure the workpiece with double-sided tape and cut out the recess ⅛" at a time.

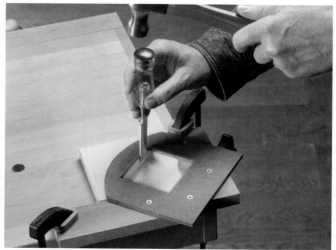

Use a chiesl to square the corners of the cutout.

CONTRIBUTORS

DEWALT
800-433-9258
WWW.DEWALT.COM

THE PINSKE EDGE
320-238-2385
WWW.PINSKE-EDGE.COM

ROCKLER COMPANIES, INC.
800-279-4441
WWW.ROCKLER.COM

SEARS
800-349-4358
WWW.SEARS.COM

INDEX

CREATIVE PUBLISHING INTERNATIONAL

Accessible Home
Open House
Lighting Design & Installation
Customizing Your Home
Building & Finishing Walls & Ceilings
Basic Wiring & Electrical Repairs
Advanced Home Wiring
Home Plumbing Projects & Repairs
Advanced Home Plumbing
Carpentry: Remodeling
Built-In Projects for the Home
Decorating With Paint & Wallcovering
Refinishing & Finishing Wood
Building Decks
Advanced Deck Building
Building Porches & Patios
Exterior Home Repairs & Improvements
Outdoor Wood Furnishings
Home Masonry Repairs & Projects
Stonework & Masonry Projects
Finishing Basements & Attics
Complete Guide to Painting & Decorating
Complete Guide to Home Plumbing
Complete Guide to Home Wiring
Complete Guide to Home Storage
Complete Guide to Building Decks
Complete Guide to Home Masonry
Complete Guide to Bathrooms
Complete Guide to Ceramic & Stone Tile
Complete Guide to Creative Landscapes
Complete Guide to Windows & Doors
Complete Guide to Flooring
Complete Guide to Kitchens
Complete Guide to Roofing & Siding
Complete Photo Guide to Home Repair
Complete Photo Guide to Home Improvement
Complete Photo Guide to Outdoor Home Improvement

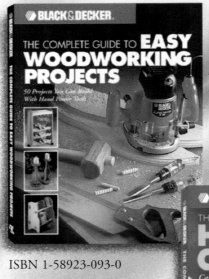

ISBN 1-58923-093-0

ISBN 0-86573-577-8

ISBN 1-58923-139-2

CREATIVE PUBLISHING INTERNATIONAL

18705 LAKE DRIVE EAST
CHANHASSEN, MN 55317

WWW.CREATIVEPUB.COM